CAREER CHOICES
for Undergraduates
Considering an

M.B.A.

by
CAREER ASSOCIATES

Walker and Company
NEW YORK

First published in the United States of America in 1985 by the Walker
Publishing Company, Inc.

Published simultaneously in Canada by John Wiley & Sons Canada,
Limited, Rexdale, Ontario.

Library of Congress Cataloging in Publication Data
Main entry under title:

Career choices for undergraduates considering an M.B.A.

  Bibliography: p.
  1. United States—Occupations. 2. College graduates—Employment—
United States. 3. Vocational guidance—United States. I. Career Associates.
HF5382.5.U5C2558 1985   331.7'023   83-40439
ISBN 0-8027-0788-2
ISBN 0-8027-7244-7 (pbk.)

Printed in the United States of America

10 9 8 7 6 5 4 3 2 1

Titles in the Series

Career Choices for Students of:
Art
Business
Communications and Journalism
Computer Science
Economics
English
History
Mathematics
Political Science and Government
Psychology

Career Choices for Undergraduates Considering:
Law
An M.B.A.

Acknowledgments

We gratefully acknowledge the help of the many people who spent time talking to our research staff about employment opportunities in their fields. This book would not have been possible without their assistance. Our thanks, too, to Catalyst, which has one of the best career libraries in the country in its New York, NY, offices. We also acknowledge the contribution of the Financial Women's Association of New York, an organization composed of professionals from various financial industries, which helped us to locate interviewees for several of the chapters in this book.

CAREER ASSOCIATES

CONTENTS

WHAT'S IN THIS BOOK FOR YOU?

In today's complex, fast-paced business world, liberal arts graduates—or even graduates with technical backgrounds in engineering or the physical sciences—often find it difficult to compete without the specialized skills that are becoming more and more necessary for a successful business career. Sophisticated analytical and quantitative skills are needed to deal effectively with the problems facing business leaders today: a changing economy, rapidly developing technology, the environmental and social effects of business decisions. Excellent managers with a broad knowledge of the business world and the techniques by which a business is run are in great demand, and will continue to be. In order to broaden their career opportunities many graduates are considering a master of business administration degree, either directly following graduation or after some time on the job.

The M.B.A. is obtained through a two-year course of study that includes such disciplines as accounting, finance, statistical analysis, organizational behavior, marketing, and operations management. Students take a series of core courses in these areas; this is the common body of business knowledge that employers know every M.B.A. has. At most schools students also take specialized courses in an area of their choice: finance, marketing, accounting, international business, information systems, and public and non-profit management are only some of the concentrations available.

There are two principal methods of instruction in M.B.A. courses: case study and theoretical. The case study approach is inductive and emphasizes problem-solving in various business situations that the student will encounter on the job. The theoretical approach teaches a conceptual framework from which students can learn to deduce solutions to business problems. Most schools' curricula employ some mixture of the two methods.

Once you have an M.B.A., however, what do you do? *Career Choices for Undergraduates Considering an M.B.A.* was designed to answer just that question. Although M.B.A.s work in every conceivable type of business enterprise, eight of the major areas in which they are employed are accounting, banking, the energy industry, the electronics industry, investment banking, manufacturing, management consulting, and securities. The book's easy-to-use format combines general information about each of these industries with the hard facts that anyone considering an M.B.A. will find indispensable.

An overall explanation of each industry is followed by authoritative material on the job outlook—the competition for the openings that exist and the new opportunities that may arise from such factors as expansion and technological development. There is a listing of employers by type and by geographic location and a sampling of leading companies by name—by no means all, but enough to give you a good idea of who the employers are. The section on how to break into the field is not general how-to-get-a-job advice, but rather zeroes in on ways of getting a foot in the door of a particular industry.

You will find a description of the major functional areas within each industry. For example, the accounting chapter discusses the differences between management, government, and public accounting. For each functional area within an industry you'll learn what your duties—both basic and more challenging—are likely to be, what hours you'll work, the workstyle, what range of salary to expect.* What personal and professional qualifications must you have? How can you move up—and to what? This book tells you.

Internships, an important way of making the contacts that will aid you in your search for full-time employment, are discussed, and you'll find a list of the books and periodicals you will want to read to keep up with latest trends in an industry you are considering. There are also names and addresses of professional associations that can be helpful to you—through student chapters, open meetings, and printed information. Finally, interviews with professionals in each field bring you the experiences of successful people who are actually working in the kinds of jobs you may be aiming for.

Many questions that must be answered will arise as you investigate the possibility of graduate business education. The information contained in this book will help you answer them—easily and definitively. But only you—through an objective assessment

---

* Salary figures given are the latest available as the book goes to press.

of your own abilities and career goals, and further research into schools and industries—can answer the ultimate question: Should I get an M.B.A.? Whatever your decision, we wish you every success in finding a rewarding work future.

ACCOUNTING

PENCILS, ledger books, endless columns of figures—a career spent with the tools of the accounting profession appeals to many business majors. With tax laws becoming more complicated and government regulations requiring more careful audits, the skills of the accountant are more in demand than ever before. Accountants design, maintain, and audit the financial records of businesses and institutions. They aid management personnel in financial planning and ensure the accuracy of all financial statements. The accountant makes a strong contribution to an organization's credibility in the eyes of investors, creditors, government agencies (particularly in regard to taxes), trade and professional association members, and contributors.

The master of business administration degree is becoming very relevant to the accounting profession. The combination of an undergraduate degree in accounting and an accounting concentration at the graduate level is an excellent preparation for a career in that field. Either an undergraduate accounting degree supplemented by a well-rounded M.B.A. program or any liberal arts degree combined with an M.B.A. concentration in accounting will make you a desirable candidate.

The M.B.A. accountant faces unusually keen competition. The accounting profession is a large one, but most entry-level jobs are not suited to the skills gained through graduate work. Those employers who do seek candidates with advanced education will often hire a person with a master's in accounting over an M.B.A. However, in all areas of the industry, the analytical skills and financial savvy of the M.B.A. are needed and jobs are available for graduates who have mastered the technical skills of accounting.

Whatever your background, you must demonstrate far more than fiscal and mathematical skills. Accountants do not work over their books in solitude; they are active participants in daily business operations. Their findings and observations must be used by others, so the would-be accountant must have exceptional organizational and communications skills. The ability to continue to learn is also a vital part of any accounting career because of ever changing tax laws and business regulations. Further education can also open up new career possibilities as your growing knowledge and experience allow you to explore new options.

Accounting professionals work in three major areas:

- **Public Accounting**
- **Management Accounting**
- **Government Accounting**

Public accounting is the most visible branch of the industry, primarily because of the status of the certified public accountant (C.P.A.). Public accountants serve client businesses by auditing their books, preparing tax returns, and advising on tax, business, investment, and related concerns. Management accountants, also known as private, internal, or industrial accountants, work within industries and businesses and with charitable, educational, and religious institutions. They handle such functions as cost analysis, budgeting, payroll, and inventory control, and offer advice on financial matters. Government accountants perform the same role, but work within the government rather than in private industry.

Information processing technologies have significantly affected the daily routines of many accounting professionals. Computers are increasingly relied on for record-keeping and financial analysis. Accountants are now able to complete many jobs more quickly without sacrificing standards of thoroughness and accuracy.

Job Outlook

Job Openings Will Grow: Faster than average

Competition for Jobs: Keen

New Job Opportunities: The expanding, complex body of tax laws confronting the business community is creating an increased demand for tax accounts. Although most accountants do some tax work, larger businesses often need the services of accountants who specialize in this area. Job experience with the Internal Revenue Service (IRS) is the best education for anyone considering a career in tax accounting, but jobs in public and management accounting can also involve the newcomer in a great deal of tax work. If you are interested in this branch of the industry, be sure to study tax law and become aware of current changes in and additions to tax regulations.

Geographic Job Index

New York, NY, Chicago, IL, Los Angeles, CA, and Washington, DC, have higher concentrations of accountants than other specific locales, but jobs are not limited to these cities. Accounting jobs may be found in all regions of the United States, mainly in urban and industrial areas.

Who the Employers Are

PUBLIC ACCOUNTING for one of the 30,000 U.S. public accounting firms can mean working in a small, one-person operation or for an international giant employing thousands. The largest are the so-called Big Eight, which have the personnel to handle major corporations as clients and, as a result, great prestige. The M.B.A. is in the highest demand at such firms.

MANAGEMENT ACCOUNTING in many businesses may require only one person handling some accounting functions, but the real career opportunities lie in firms large enough to need the expertise of the M.B.A. You might also find work in service industries, such as hospitals and universities. Here you may work alone or with small staff and will be almost exclusively concerned with financial planning and analysis, rather than with the daily routine of basic accounting.

GOVERNMENT employs accounting staffs in departments and agencies at the federal, state, county, and municipal levels, smaller governmental units, such as townships and boroughs, often hire public accounting firms to handle their books. Although job opportunities for M.B.A. accountants are more limited here than in public and management accounting, you will find some demand for your education.

Major Employers

THE BIG EIGHT

Arthur Andersen & Company, Chicago IL
Arthur Young & Company, New York, NY
Coopers & Lybrand, New York, NY
Deloitte, Haskins & Sells, New York, NY
Ernst & Whinney, Cleveland, OH
Peat, Marwick, Mitchell & Company, New York, NY
Price Waterhouse & Company, New York, NY
Touche Ross & Company, New York, NY
These companies have branches throughout the country.

GOVERNMENT departments employing the largest numbers of accountants and auditors are:

Department of Agriculture
Department of Defense Audit Agencies
Department of Energy
Department of Health and Human Services
Department of the Air Force
Department of the Army
Department of the Navy
General Accounting Office
Treasury Department (includes the Internal Revenue
    Service)

How to Break into the Field

Because of keen competition for jobs with the Big Eight, you need a strong grade point average and a high class standing. These firms recruit at business schools, as do other large employers of public accountants. However, because most public accounting firms do not have recruitment personnel, your best bet is to make your own investigation through personal referrals and newspapers advertisements.

Large businesses also recruit management accountants. Keep an eye on the classified ads and make direct applications to companies that interest you.

You must apply for government accounting jobs in the same way as for any other government job. At the federal level, contact the nearest job information center for application details. Most federal applicants must go through the Office of Personnel Management, but some departments, such as the Department of Defense, have their own personnel offices. In either case, you must submit the standard federal application form, SF-171, and a college transcript. With an M.B.A., you would apply only for management-level positions that require specific skills. Normally, the federal government promotes from within, but occasionally openings appear that cannot be filled without looking for outside talent. The M.B.A. is also sought by a few agencies, such as the

Securities and Exchange Commission (SEC), that specifically recruit personnel with advanced degrees and/or work experience. After your application is received, your qualifications are evaluated and you are given a numerical rating. When your number reaches the head of a list of qualified candidates for the position that interests you, you will be interviewed. If the job is in another part of the country and you are willing to relocate—always an important consideration when applying for federal work—you may be interviewed on the phone. The entry-level rating for an M.B.A. graduate on the federal pay schedule is GS-9.

Application requirements with smaller government bodies vary. Contact state, county, or local government personnel agencies to learn their needs for applicants with advanced degrees.

International Job Opportunities

The largest public accounting firms and corporations have overseas branches, but these are staffed by foreign nationals in most areas. An exception is the Middle East, where Americans who are fluent in Arabic are needed.

PUBLIC ACCOUNTING

The most important function of the public accountant is auditing. This includes an inspection of the client's internal operations, records and documents and, possibly, company employees on the job. The auditor inspects procedures for bill paying, inventory control, and other financial operations and establishes the balances of income, debts, assets, and investments. Auditors base their final reports on their observations, experience, and knowledge of sound business practices. A background in economics and business administration is valuable in this respect. Auditors must also be able to exercise good judgment.

The audit gives clients a complete and accurate assessment of their financial standing; it aids management in planning and protects investors and stockholders. An annual audit is mandatory for all publicly held corporations.

Many businesses and organizations, even those with internal accounting departments, hire public accountants to prepare tax returns. These clients see a distinct advantage in having an objective agency perform this important task. In such cases, the public accountant adopts the role of tax adviser.

Some businesses also engage public accountants to provide advice on investments and accounting procedures, performing for small firms the same functions as internal accountants in larger businesses.

Certified public accountants receive greater recognition than other public accountants, both from the public and from other accounting professionals. You are awarded certification once you have demonstrated your mastery of accounting skills in a five-part examination. The exam tests accounting theory, commercial law, and accounting techniques. A standard national test is used, but it is administrated by state boards of accountancy, which may set their own requirements. All sections of the test need not be taken in one sitting, and any sections not passed may be retaken. But the time period in which you must pass the complete exam varies from state to state. Some states also require a minimum amount of work experience as a public accountant before awarding the certificate. To check the standards of the state in which you plan to practice, consult that state's board of accountancy or the American Institute of Certified Public Accountants (AICPA).

To begin preparing for the exam while still in school, pay particular attention to courses in accounting theory. This material is learned only in an academic environment; many C.P.A.s recommend that this section be taken first, before your classroom knowledge is obscured by time.

The advantages of holding the C.P.A. are many; it serves as tangible proof of your skill and your commitment to the profession. Public accounting firms, particularly the largest, often expect their accountants to receive certification as quickly as state law allows.

Beyond the entry level, the C.P.A. is often a requirement for advancement. Employers, even those in management and government accounting, prefer to see a C.P.A. when hiring an individual with public accounting experience. In private industry, C.P.A.s tend to be better paid than their noncertified counterparts. Although a varied career is possible without the certificate, having it opens a multitude of otherwise unavailable opportunities.

In most large public accounting firms, such as those of the Big Eight, you begin your job with a formal training period—generally a few weeks—to acquaint yourself with your employer's standards and practices. Even with an M.B.A., you will probably work at first with employees who have only an undergraduate degree. The M.B.A. does not spare you from the daily chores of the staff accountant, but because of your knowledge and experience, you will be promoted quickly. When recruiting M.B.A.s, major public accounting firms are looking for individuals who have the potential to become partners—the executives who run a public accounting firm. Only some 2 percent of those hired as staff accountants reach the level of partner, so if you get to be a partner you are joining a select group of people who have the ability to be both good accountants and good administrators.

Qualifications

Personal: Good concentration. Patience. Accuracy and attention to detail. Flexibility. Objectivity. Ability to judge and make decisions. Reliability.

Professional: Writing and communications skills. Exceptional mathematical ability. Commitment to professional standards. Ability to work independently.

Career Paths

LEVEL	JOB TITLE	EXPERIENCE NEEDED
Entry	Staff or junior accountant	M.B.A.; work experience often preferred

2	Senior accountant	1-3 years
3	Manager	3-5 years
4	Partner	8 + years

Job Responsibilities

Entry Level

THE BASICS: Preparing a client's books. Performing transactional tests (these verify the accuracy of bookkeeping procedures). Preparing tax returns.

MORE CHALLENGING DUTIES: Offering your recommendations and opinions on sections of an audit to senior personnel. Doing background research. Learning tax law. Meeting with clients.

Moving Up

Promotion in any size firm depends on your competence in accounting techniques and procedures. Senior accountants are responsible for the transactional tests that ensure the accuracy of your findings. At the entry level you may be asked your opinion of an audit's findings, but only experienced personnel report directly to a client. Managers oversee the largest audits and service clients. The partners are the owners/executives of a public accounting firm, and are ultimately responsible for all decisions concerning the firm and its clients. They also solicit new accounts. You must be invited to become a partner and, in some cases, may have to buy into the firm.

Solo practice is an option open to experienced accountants. The advantage of working alone or starting your own small firm is that you may be selective in your choice of accounts. However, only a highly organized individual can successfully handle solo practice.

MANAGEMENT ACCOUNTING

Management accountants handle internal financial record-keeping; provide data on investments, taxes, budgets, and cost analysis; and aid executive personnel in financial decision-making. These duties sound similar to those of public accountants with good reason—many businesses employ public accountants only to conduct audits; in-house staff handle all other accounting functions. Other organizations divide their accounting needs between public and management accounting, giving some functions, such as taxes, to an outside firm and assign day-to-day jobs, such as payroll and budgeting, to the internal staff. For this reason, the career paths and duties of management accountants vary considerably.

The general accounting department handles daily business needs, such as payroll, budgeting, accounts receivable, accounts payable, general ledger, and financial statements. In smaller firms, the title general accountant might be held by the individual who handles or directs most or all accounting functions. This individual would, in turn, work most closely with public account-ants if the organization employs them.

General accountants must pay close attention to all laws and regulations affecting daily business operations.They are involved in sending out all payments, royalties, dividends, rents, and other necessary expenditures. General accountants also offer advice on affordability of purchases and services.

Tax accountants prepare tax returns and must be extremely knowledgeable about federal, state, and local tax laws. For this reason, many tax accountants have prior experience in public or government accounting. Senior accountants are responsible for seeing that the organization conforms to all tax laws.

Cost accountants determine the cost of goods and services. Their work is needed by manufacturing and service industries alike. They are instrumental in determining prices that are high enough to ensure a profit but low enough to interest consumers. Cost accountants work with marketing and manufacturing staffs, and some familiarity with the work of these departments is helpful.

Internal auditing is a specialized area of management account-ing that has attracted a great deal of interest in recent years. Because of the growing body of federal legislation concerning business accounting standards and public access to information about corporate finances, internal auditing has changed from the luxury it once was to an absolute necessity. The internal auditor conducts an independent appraisal from within the organization by analyzing, criticizing, and recommending improvements to inter-nal financial practices. The internal auditor also ensures the safety and profitability of investments and assets, and seeks to uncover sources of waste and inefficiency. By virtue of being inside the organization, the internal auditor is privy to confidential informa-tion that is not shared with auditing public accountants.

In addition to being a skilled accountant, the internal auditor must have a comprehensive understanding of all fundamental business areas: marketing, manufacturing, advertising, and stock-holder relations. Internal auditing is an excellent path to an execu-tive position because of the background provided by this exposure. However, despite the thrill of investigation, internal auditing is largely a job of long hours and repetitive work; one must be an individual of exceptional diligence and concentration.

An M.B.A. is a requirement for going into a specialized area of management accounting—financial planning and analysis. Finan-cial planners are concerned with the budgetary and financial needs of an organization, investigating expenditures, profits, cash flow, and investments. They offer financial advice on the effects of mergers and corporate growth and may have the power to reject or discourage major expenditures and investments.

The management accounting end of the industry is aware of the need to demonstrate a commitment to high professional standards. Certification is now available to management accountants: the Certificate in Management Accounting (C.M.A.) and the Certified Internal Auditor (C.I.A.). The C.M.A. exam is sponsored by the National Association of Accountants and tests decision-making capability and knowledge of business law, finance, and organiza-tion. The C.I.A. exam is sponsored by the Institute of Internal

Auditors and tests the theory and practice of internal auditing. Work experience is required for certification. Multiple certification is permissible and encouraged.

Qualifications

Personal: Reliability. Ability to work independently. Flexibility. Discipline.

Professional: Understanding of business and the marketplace. Willingness to increase your knowledge of practical accounting techniques.

Career Paths

LEVEL	JOB TITLE	EXPERIENCE NEEDED
Entry	Staff accountant	M.B.A.; work experience often preferred
2	Senior accountant	1-3 years
3	General accountant, manager of tax accounting, cost analysis, etc., chief internal auditor	4-8 years
4	Treasurer, controller, chief financial officer	10+ years

Job Responsibilities

Entry Level

THE BASICS: Bookkeeping. Writing and recording checks. Filling out tax returns. Keeping files.

MORE CHALLENGING DUTIES: Offering your ideas on improved accounting procedures. Helping to prepare reports on company finances. Learning about the accounting department's relationship with other sections of the organization.

Moving Up

As an M.B.A. graduate, you will be expected to demonstrate an understanding of the financial operations of the company or organization as a whole. Your background and skills will determine the positions for which you are suited, but, in general, M.B.A.s are sought for such functions, as financial analysis and internal auditing, where analytical and organizational abilities take precedence over the technical skills of accounting. With an M.B.A., you can expect to move eventually into such executive roles as controller, treasurer, and chief financial officer.

The controller is the executive in charge of all accounting functions and summarizes financial information for executive personnel. This individual must have a keen understanding of all business operations and the judgment to make financial planning decisions. The treasurer handles the cash flow and all financial reserves and is involved with loans, credit, and investments. Many firms combine the functions of controller and treasurer into one position.

The chief financial officer oversees the controller, treasurer, chief internal auditor, and the accounting staffs. He or she advises top executives as to the financial needs and stability of the organization. The chief financial officer does not have to be an accountant, but often this individual has accounting experience. That top financial management can rise from the ranks of accountants demonstrates the importance of the accounting department in overall policy-making.

GOVERNMENT ACCOUNTING

Government accounting attracts those graduates and experienced accountants who want to use the skills of management accounting in a different setting. Government agencies tend to pay less than private industry, but as an employer, government offers distinct advantages: job security, excellent benefits, and some unique opportunities. The goal of the accounting department of a typical government agency is to function within the budgetary constraints mandated by legislative action. If government service interests you, keep in mind that it is primarily the federal government, which offers some unique options, that will want you, not state or local governments.

The IRS is the single largest employer of accountants in the United States. The IRS particularly needs accounting graduates to be agents—the people on the receiving end of federal tax returns. This job requires strong accounting abilities and the temperament to work with taxpayers.

IRS work requires extensive entry-level training. You begin with an orientation and seven weeks of classroom training covering all aspects of tax law, fraud examination, and research techniques. Then, under the guidance of professionals, you continue your training on the job by reviewing simple taxpayer returns. Next, you receive classroom training on the examination of corporate tax returns and work with such returns. Finally, you are instructed in handling the more complex corporate returns, learning about tax shelters and other intricacies of tax law.

As you progress, you might remain a tax generalist, specialize in the returns of a particular industry, or be called on to instruct new trainees. Investigations or special projects might also require your participation.

The SEC offers excellent opportunities for experienced C.P.A.s who have at least three years of experience working with publicly held corporations in a public accounting firm. The SEC regulates all firms that sell stock by developing general accounting and auditing regulations and reviewing such companies' compliance with these regulations. After analyzing an audit of a particular corporation, the SEC may call for an investigation.

The army has centralized its accounting staff at the United States Army Finance Accounting Center, located at Fort Benjamin Harrison in Indianapolis, IN. Job openings exist for both operations accountants, who handle daily accounting needs, and systems accountants, who develop computer-based accounting systems for military bases and offices. Once you are employed by the federal government, you can transfer to other departments and agencies. You may move to a similar position, or to one with greater responsibilities. Current employees ("status employees," as they are called) receive preference in all hiring decisions.

Opportunities at state and local levels vary, but the greatest need for accountants is normally found in the larger departments and agencies, such as those handling transportation and road maintenance, law enforcement, and tax collection.

ADDITIONAL INFORMATION

Salaries

Salaries vary according to the employer's size. The following ranges for starting annual salaries are taken from Robert Haft International's 1984 study. This study did not include holders of M.B.A. degrees. M.B.A.s can expect to earn salaries at the high end of these ranges, and possibly more. You will certainly be better paid than an employee in a comparable position who does not hold an advanced degree.

PUBLIC ACCOUNTING
Entry level $16,500 to $19,000
                                           (medium-size firm)
                                           $18,000 to $20,000
                                           (large firm)

1-3 years experience	$18,000 to $23,000 (medium) $20,000 to $24,500 (large)
Senior	$23,000 to $32,000 (medium) $24,000 to $34,000 (large)
Manager	$33,000 to $46,000 (medium) $36,000 to $56,000 (large)

MANAGEMENT ACCOUNTING

Entry level	$15,000 to $17,000 (medium-size firm) $15,000 to $18,000 (large firm)
1-3 years experience	$23,000 to $28,500 (medium) $18,000 to $26,000 (large)
Senior	$23,000 to $28,000 (medium) $27,000 to $31,000 (large)
Manager	$29,000 to $34,000 (medium) $33,000 to $50,000 (large)

GOVERNMENT ACCOUNTING

Government accountants are paid according to standard pay scales. For federal salaries, consult the Office of Personnel Management for current figures.

Working Conditions

Hours: Accounting is a nine-to-five job, except during tax season. The workload during this period—roughly December to May—is especially heavy for public accountants and tax accountants. Expect long hours, weekend work, and no time off.

Environment: Accounting is an office job, but surroundings vary from employer to employer. At the entry level you might share an office, have a desk in a general work area,or, at large businesses and public accounting firms, enjoy the luxury of a private office from the beginning. As you progress, your surroundings become more comfortable. Management accountants work in the administrative offices of their organizations. As an accountant for the Department of Defense, you might work as a civilian on a military base.

Workstyle: Most work is done at your desk, but public accountants frequently work at clients' offices. Management and government accountants generally have fewer opportunities to work out of the office.

Travel: Travel opportunities exist for many accounting professionals. Even in small public accounting firms, overnight travel may be required for visits to clients. In large firms, such as those of the Big Eight, you might spend days or weeks away on a single project. In management accounting, internal auditing staffers are most likely to travel; in multinational corporations this can mean international travel for experienced personnel. Certain federal departments, such as the Department of Defense, require extensive national and international travel.

Recommended Reading

BOOKS

The Big Eight by Mark Stevens, Macmillan Publishing Company: 1981

How to Speak Accounting: A Glossary of Terms with Guidance on How to Read an Annual Report by Sidney Davidson and Clyde P. Stickney, Harcourt Brace Jovanovich: 1983

The Modern Accountant's Handbook, edited by James D. Edwards and Homer A. Black, Dow-Jones-Irwin: 1976

PERIODICALS

CPA Journal (monthly), New York Society of Certified Public Accountants, 600 Third Avenue, New York, NY 10016

Government Accountants Journal (quarterly), Association of Government Accountants, 727 South 23rd Street, Arlington, VA 22202

Journal of Accountancy (monthly), American Institute of Certified Public Accountants, 1211 Avenue of the Americas, New York, NY 10036

Management Accounting (monthly), National Association of Accountants, 919 Third Avenue, New York, NY 10022

The Practical Accountant (monthly), Warren, Gorham, and Lamont, Inc., 210 South Street, Boston, MA 02111

The Wall Street Journal (daily), 23 Cortlandt Street, New York, NY 10007

Professional Associations

American Institute of Certified Public Accountants
1211 Avenue of the Americas
New York, NY 10036

American Society of Women Accountants
35 East Wacker Drive
Chicago, IL 60601

Association of Government Accountants
727 South 23rd Street
Arlington, VA 22202

Institute of Internal Auditors
249 Maitland Avenue
Altamonte Springs, FL 32701

National Association of Accountants
919 Third Avenue
New York, NY 10022

INTERVIEW

Richard Lemieux, Age 34
Manager
Ernst & Whinney, Cleveland, OH

The business environment has always fascinated me—even in high
school I kept abreast of the stock market—so naturally I studied
business administration in college. I was interested in a career that
would be different from the usual nine-to-five routine—a profession that would provide challenge and opportunity. An internship
with a Big Eight firm convinced me that public accounting was a
profession I would enjoy.

The combination of a master's degree (M.B.A.) and the internship experience gave me an advantage in the job market. I started with Ernst & Whinney at a step above the entry-level position because of these qualifications, and shortly thereafter I obtained my C.P.A. certificate. The public accounting environment has more than met my requirements for a rewarding career. I work in a flexible environment; the hours are not rigid, unlike in some other professions, but they can be long and demanding. I like the variety of engagements and special projects, and I particularly enjoy working with our clients. After ten years with Ernst & Whinney, I can honestly say I enjoy every new day.

Careers in public accounting present challenges that are not always associated with accounting. For example, many of our staff people are now working with microcomputers in order to explore their applications to the audit environment. The requirements for tax research seem to increase daily, and in the consulting area our people are involved with feasibility studies, cash flow projections, and financial forecasting.

At the present time, I am serving a tour of duty through Ernst & Whinney's national office in Cleveland, OH. This opportunity allowed me to transfer from our Portland, MA, office to work in an environment that is very different from anything I thought I'd be doing. I am now involved in nonclient capacity, meaning that my job is part of the internal functions of our national office. Specifically, I am serving as a manager in the national personnel group, dealing mostly with the administration of personnel policy, corporate relocation, recruiting, and personnel information systems. I am also directly involved with the Ernst & Whinney Foundation, which is responsible for our firm's matching gift program as well as other grants and endowments to colleges and universities. I thoroughly enjoy this opportunity to work in the national office, but must admit that I miss having direct contact with our clients. After my tour of duty is over, I will return to one of our practice offices to continue working as a C.P.A. in the accounting and auditing environment.

BANKING

IMAGINE yourself the manager of an operations department, responsible for the global transfer of currencies worth several million dollars. Or a member of the international department, traveling to the Middle East, Africa, or Europe to check on overseas branches. Or managing a loan portfolio for a major multinational corporation, providing their chief financial officer with up-to-date financial information. Banking has become the central nervous system of the world's economy, and today's dynamic banker can be found in front of a desktop terminal calling up the vast amount of financial data needed to provide an increasing array of new products and services. Today customers not only want banks to be the safekeepers and lenders of money, they also want banks to provide brokerage services and electronic funds transfers. If you want to be involved in a state-of-the-art business, if you have an entrepreneurial spirit, and, above all, if you are endowed with keen creativity, a career in banking is for you.

The changes in banking are primarily due to the impact of technology. Banking is now a worldwide 24-hour-a-day business. Automated teller machines, home banking via microcomputers, and office automation have affected every bank employee. But you don't have to be a whiz kid who talks in bits and bytes to get your foot in the door. Every major bank has either a formal training program or professional on-the-job training that includes instruction in the use of the technology. What is most important is your ability to grasp the concepts and quickly master the skills.

More and more students entering the field have had the foresight to make themselves knowledgeable about telecommunications in order to gain an understanding of the newly diverse world of banking. These students have a better chance of getting a job offer than those with a limited, traditional view of the industry.

The industry welcomes M.B.A. graduates from a wide variety of backgrounds. Graduate concentrations in finance, marketing, and accounting are often preferred, but any M.B.A. concentration is acceptable. Your undergraduate major is of less concern to employers. A candidate with a liberal arts background may enter the industry as easily as one with an undergraduate degree in a business-related discipline.

Most banks put all new employees through a training program. Some M.B.A.s, depending on their backgrounds and their employers' policies, will not be placed in a formal training program, but will receive their orientation on the job. Simply having an M.B.A. will not spare you from performing routine entry-level duties, but you can expect to gain responsibility and receive your first promotion much more quickly than non-M.B.A., entry-level employees.

Commercial banking recruits M.B.A.s chiefly for the following functional areas:

- **Credit Lending**
- **Operations**
- **Systems**
- **Trusts**

Job Outlook

Job Openings Will Grow: Faster than average

Competition for Jobs: Keen
Expect the most competition for positions in credit lending. Expanding opportunities can be found in the operations and systems areas. As new sources for loans become harder to find, operations is being looked to for development of fee-based services, such as letters of credit and money transfer services. In systems, the computerization and communications systems needed to deliver customer services are implemented.

New Job Opportunities: Because of industry deregulation, banks are now actively seeking people to work in such diverse areas as mergers and acquisitions, private banking (which serves individuals with high net worth and high incomes), office automation (which develops executive information systems and implements them throughout the bank), product management (which includes the planning, pricing, and marketing of new products and services) and telecommunications (which develops the global communications channels necessary for getting and submitting information).

The skills of the M.B.A. are specifically needed in specialized areas, such as international banking and multinational corporate accounts, that require exceptional analytical skills and the ability to handle unusually large and complex problems.

Geographic Job Index

Although banks can be found in any city or town, the major money centers are located in New York, NY, Chicago, IL, San Francisco, CA, and Boston, MA. Opportunities at the regional or local end of the industry are growing in Dallas, TX, Houston, TX, and other cities in the Southwest.

Who the Employers Are

COMMERCIAL BANKS (or money-center banks) market their products and services to multinational corporations, smaller banks (called correspondents), and individuals (who use checking and loan services).

REGIONAL BANKS provide many of the same services as the larger money-center banks, but on a smaller scale. Their clients are typically locally based small and medium-size businesses.

SAVINGS AND LOAN ASSOCIATIONS offer their customers personal savings accounts and mortgages. However, under new banking legislation they are allowed to make commercial and business loans.

Major Employers

COMMERCIAL BANKS

> Bank of America, San Francisco, CA
> Bankers Trust Company, New York, NY
> Chase Manhattan Bank, New York, NY
> Chemical Bank, New York, NY
> Citibank, New York, NY
> Continental Illinois National Bank, Chicago, IL
> First National Bank of Boston, Boston, MA
> First National Bank of Chicago, Chicago, IL
> Manufacturers Hanover Trust Company, New York, NY
> Security Pacific National Bank, Los Angeles, CA

REGIONAL BANKS

> First Bank System, Minneapolis, MN
> Mellon Bank, Pittsburgh, PA
> Mercantile Bank, St. Louis, MO
> NCNB National Bank, Charlotte, NC
> Ranier National Bank, Seattle, WA
> Republic Bank Dallas, Dallas, TX
> Wachovia Bank & Trust Company, Winston-Salem, NC

How to Break into the Field

Do not wait until after you have your M.B.A. to investigate banking. Many banks are eager to have business school students participate in summer internships; this experience is required by a few employers and preferred by most. If you choose to become a full-time employee at the bank and in the department in which you were an intern, you may move more quickly through training or bypass it completely.

Before any interview—whether it is for an internship or a full-time job—do your homework. Learn all you can about the internal workings of the area in which you plan to interview. If your field of interest is not represented, select the next most appropriate area and ask the recruiter to forward your résumé to the proper section. Also learn something about the bank itself. Different banks have different personalities. Some are aggressive, others more traditional and conservative. Try to interview with banks whose corporate identity is compatible with your own.

International Job Opportunities

The chance to work overseas does exist in banks with international operations. If you are interested in working abroad, you should apply to work in the international department. There you may have the opportunity to alternate assignments of perhaps three to five years abroad with stints in the United States. Competence in a foreign language is helpful but not a requirement because your employer will provide language instruction.

With international experience you might eventually become involved in financial consulting, working with corporations and governments. With international debts soaring, international banking has become a challenging, dynamic area that needs the best and the brightest.

CREDIT LENDING

This is the most visible area of banking and includes the traditional bank-client relationship that almost everyone associates with the industry. However, there is more to this aspect of banking than just extending credit or offering interest-bearing accounts to clients. In consumer banking, a lending officer assesses the creditworthiness of individuals. In commercial banking, officers evaluate the financial status of corporations or nonprofit organizations; perform industry surveys, analyzing a particular industry to determine if backing a firm in that area is a good loan risk; make production forecasts to see if a borrowing firm's available resources will meet production requirements; predict how a loan would affect positively or negatively the bank's cash flow; or handle corporate overdrafts, contacting corporate customers whose payments are not on time.

During training you will go on customer calls with experienced loan officers and be responsible for taking notes and writing a report on the customer and the loan review, not as a participant but as an observer. You may be called on to research new business prospects, making cold calls to prospects in a given territory or industry. Your responsibilities will soon grow broader, and you will begin making decisions on modest loans.

Qualifications

Personal: Strong analytical skills. Ability to conceptualize. An affinity for quantitative problems. Strong negotiation skills. Extremely good interpersonal skills.

Professional: Ability to analyze data and financial statements and do creative financial planning. Familiarity with bank products and services. Ability to present clearly written reports.

Career Paths

LEVEL	JOB TITLE	EXPERIENCE NEEDED
Entry	Trainee	M.B.A., internship experience often preferred
2	Assistant loan officer	6 months-1 year
3	Loan officer/branch manager	2-4 years
4	Loan manager	5+ years

Job Responsibilities

Entry Level

THE BASICS: Training will consist of both classroom instruction in finance, accounting, credit analysis, and so forth, and actual account work, helping lending officers make judgments about existing or potential bank relationships.

MORE CHALLENGING DUTIES: Upon completion of training, you will be assigned to a line lending area, attend advanced banking seminars, and have the opportunity to meet with customers.

Moving Up

Your advancement will depend on your ability to establish advantageous client relationships, the successful closing of lucrative loan deals, and knowing when not to approve a loan. As you advance, the loan review process will become more complex and involve significantly more money. You can measure your success by your approval authority—how big a loan you are authorized to approve without going to a higher level of management.

OPERATIONS

The most successful banks anticipate and satisfy all their customers' financial needs. Operations occupies a front-row seat in the banking industry because it has bankwide responsibility for providing customers with fee-based (nonloan) services—letters of credit, money transfers, and foreign exchange services are of increased importance because banks can no longer make the profits they once did by lending money to customers. The operations department is usually the largest department of a commercial bank. Chase Manhattan Bank's operations department, for example, has more than 4000 employees. The length of your training depends on how much exposure you have had to bank operations. You will move into a supervisory position, managing the clerical staff, with responsibility for setting up assignments and time schedules, evaluating performance, making sure work is done properly, training new employees, authorizing salary increases. Work in operations also involves trouble-shooting for customers; for example, solving an account problem by tracing a money transfer that was never credited.

Qualifications

Personal: Ability to meet deadlines. Ability to perform under pressure. Ability to get along with many different types of people.

Professional: Ability to understand and follow through on complex instructions. Familiarity with concepts of computer science or a related discipline. Knowledge of fee-based services and products.

Career Paths

LEVEL	JOB TITLE	EXPERIENCE NEEDED
Entry	Operations	M.B.A., prior experience often preferred
2	Supervisor	Up to 1 year
3	Department manager	2-3 years
4	Division manager	5+ years

Job Responsibilities

Entry Level

THE BASICS: You begin your career in operations either in a formal training program, or, more likely, on the job. You will be an operations trainee for about 18 months, learning by rotating among the various departments that handle fee-based services.

MORE CHALLENGING DUTIES: After the training period, you will be assigned to a department or a staff area such as financial management or budget coordination and will learn about a single product or area in depth.

Moving Up

Your progress will depend on your ability to improve the overall productivity of your department or area, to motivate your staff, to stay within your budget, and to complete transactions efficiently and accurately. Because operations is not exclusively devoted to production management, for further advancement you will need to learn about product development, marketing and systems functions. Those who move into these areas often accompany loan officers on customer calls, offering the technical advice that will help clinch a deal, or presenting a plan to customize an existing product to meet the expanding needs of the client.

With hard work and diligence you can acquire the knowledge and expertise that will enable you to move almost anywhere in the bank organization. Operations managers can move into marketing positions, the systems areas, or perhaps relocate (even overseas) to manage a branch office.

SYSTEMS

The systems area is now involved in every banking decision from credit lending to recruitment. Most large commercial banks have both a central systems area and separate decentralized systems units that service the major components of the organization. Systems is responsible for developing, implementing, and maintaining automated programs for clients and in-house use, for selecting hardware, writing software, and consulting with the user/client when there is a need to develop special programs. In addition, systems staffers must keep up with the latest developments in technological applications and services.

Qualifications

Personal: Ability to think in analytical terms. Ease in working with abstract models.

Professional: Quantitative skills. Familiarity with the business applications of software and hardware. Ability to convert technical language and concepts into familiar and understandable terms.

Career Paths

LEVEL	JOB TITLE	EXPERIENCE NEEDED
Entry	Systems trainee	M.B.A., prior experience in banking or business computing often preferred
2	Systems analyst	1 year
3	Systems consultant	2-3 years
4	Senior systems consultant	4-5 years

Job Responsibilities

Entry Level

THE BASICS: In either a structured training program or through on-the-job training, you will become familiar with the bank's hardware and software and how they are used. You will be placed on a systems team project, refining the use of current equipment or developing systems for as yet unmet needs.

MORE CHALLENGING DUTIES: Applying your skills to more difficult or specialized projects.

Moving Up

If you demonstrate interpersonal skills as well as technical ability, you could become a project manager, overseeing a team of systems people working on the development and implementation of a specific systems capability, such as a new internal telephone switching system, or software for an executive workstation, which could include features such as electronic mail and word processing.

The potential for a talented systems person is excellent. You could end up managing an operations or office automation department, developing and installing new systems, or becoming a systems consultant for overseas branches. Successful systems personnel can move into any department in the bank.

TRUSTS

The trust department manages and invests money, property or other assets owned by a client. The pension plans of large corporations and other organizations often use trusts, as do individuals with large assets. Many estates, by the provisions of a will, are also managed in trust. This department, like the credit department, deals closely and extensively with clients. The training program is similar to that in other areas of banking, but in general advancement is slower and requires more experience.

Qualifications

Personal: A straightforward manner. Accuracy. Good with numbers. Patience in dealing with people. Confidence.

Professional: Strong analytical ability. Good business judgment. Ability to apply financial theory to practical problems.

Career Paths

LEVEL	JOB TITLE	EXPERIENCE NEEDED
Entry	Trainee	M.B.A., banking experience often preferred

2	Assistant trust officer	1-2 years
3	Trust officer	3-6 years
4	Senior trust officer	10+ years

Job Responsibilities

Entry Level

THE BASICS: Developing a familiarity with bank policies and procedures.

MORE CHALLENGING DUTIES: Researching investments, real estate, or the overall economy in order to assist superiors. Some contact with clients.

Moving Up

Showing sound judgment and an ability to work independently will garner an assignment to manage some of the smaller trust funds. Moving up also depends on your ability to attract new customers to the bank, as well as to keep present clients satisfied. As you advance you will become responsible for handling more and more money. Top level trust officers are expected not only to bring in substantial new business and to handle the largest accounts, but also to manage and support lower level employees.

ADDITIONAL INFORMATION

Salaries

Annual salaries vary according to the size of the bank. The following figures are taken from Robert Half International's 1984 survey.

Installment loans/assistant manager: $18,000 to $22,000
(small); $21,000 to $27,000 (medium); $23,000 to
$28,500 (large).

Commercial loans/branch manager: $18,000 to $22,000
(small); $21,000 to $27,000 (medium); $23,000 to
$28,500 (large).

Senior loan officer: $28,000 to $33,000 (small); $33,000 to
$37,000 (medium); $33,000 to $50,000 (large).

Mortgage loans: $23,500 to $32,000 (small); $28,000 to
$36,000 (medium); $32,000 to $41,000 (large).

Operations officer: $17,000 to $21,000 (small); $22,000 to
$29,000 (medium); $24,000 to $31,000 (large).

Trust officer: $22,000 to $29,500 (small); $23,000 to
$30,000 (medium); $27,500 to $40,000 (large).

Working Conditions

Hours: The credit trainee rarely sees daylight, because long
hours and weekend work are often required to get through the
training program. After training, normal hours will be whatever it
takes to get the job done (nine-to-five plus). The hours in operations are different because it is a 24-hour-a-day shop. Night
shifts and weekend work may be unavoidable, especially for less
experienced employees. Systems staffers may also work on a
24-hour clock; the hours are longest when new systems are being
installed and deadlines must be met.

Environment: Lending officers get the choicest locations in the
bank; because their job is customer-oriented, the surroundings are
usually plush and pleasant. The operations and systems de-

partments take a 360-degree turn from the lending department; the workspace is strictly functional, with few amenities.

Workstyle: In credit, much time is spent researching facts and figures about existing and prospective clients, which could take you from the bank library to the client's headquarters. The rest of your time will largely be spent in conference with senior lending officers. Operations and systems work is desk work. Managers walk the area, talking with the staff and lending assistance. In both of these departments, senior people may meet occasionally with systems consultants.

Travel: Travel is rare for entry-level employees in any bank. Later, however, lending officers in consumer banking might travel throughout their state. In commercial banking, research could take a lending officer to major cities throughout the country. If you are assigned to the international department in credit, operations, or systems, you might be sent to overseas branches.

Internships

Ample internship opportunities are available for the M.B.A. who is interested in a banking career. You should investigate internship openings—both the department in which you intern and the bank for which you work—as carefully as you would look for a full-time job. Many banks recruit on campus for interns, but you should also make inquiries on your own to those that do not.

Recommended Reading

BOOKS

All You Need to Know About Banks by John Cook and Robert Wood, Bantam Books: 1983

The Bankers by Martin Mayer, Ballantine Books: 1980

In Banks We Trust by Penny Lernoux, Doubleday & Company: 1984

Money and Banking by Richard W. Lindholm, Littlefield, Adams & Company: 1969

Money: Bank of the Eighties by Dimitris Chorafas, Petrocelli: 1981

The New Age of Banking by George Sterne, Profit Ideas: 1981

Polk's World Bank Directory R. L. Polk and Company

Your Career in Banking by American Bankers Association, American Bankers Association: 1980

PERIODICALS

ABA Banking Journal (monthly), 345 Hudson Street, New York, NY 10014

American Banker (daily), 1 State Street Plaza, New York, NY 10004

The Banker's Magazine (bimonthly), Warren, Gorham, and Lamont, Inc., 210 South Street, Boston, MA 02111

Bank News (monthly), 912 Baltimore Avenue, Kansas City, MO 64105

Professional Associations

American Bankers Association
1120 Connecticut Avenue, N.W.
Washington, DC 20036

Consumer Bankers Association
1725 K Street, N.W.
Washington, DC 20006

National Association of Bank Women
111 East Wacker Drive
Chicago, IL 60601

United States League of Savings Associations
111 East Wacker Drive
Chicago, IL 60601

INTERVIEWS

Jayne Geisler, Age 32
Vice President, Market and Financial Planning
Chemical Bank, New York, NY

After receiving a B.A. degree in mathematics and French in 1973 from the State University College of New York at Potsdam, I entered the M.S. teaching program at Boston College, which combined coursework with a part-time teaching position in high school mathematics. Finding teaching unchallenging and realizing my abilities would be better utilized in the business environment, I entered banking, an industry where I felt I could capitalize on my quantitative background.

I joined Chemical Bank in 1974 as a financial analyst in the finance, then control, division. My responsiblities included cost accounting and financial management reporting for the consumer banking and Upstate Regions of the Metropolitan (New York) Division. Specifically this consisted of preparing, analyzing, and monitoring the financial performance of these business segments against budget and prior years, plus the development of unit and product costs of various banking services. The work was entirely hands-on, with no formal training program, and provided me with a broad understanding of the mechanics of the banking industry.

In 1977 I transferred to the controller's area of the metropolitan division where my duties expanded to include performance reporting and analysis for the commercial as well as consumer lending areas of the division, acting as a liaison with these areas, plus coordinating their annual budgets. In addition, I was charged with designing and implementing a management information system for evaluating the financial performance of these business segments against budget.

Since 1975 I had been working toward my M.B.A. in finance at night from New York University. Coming from a nonbusiness educational background, I felt that it was apparent that an M.B.A. was necessary to enhance my professional development and my future career goals. It provided me with an understanding of the interrelationships among the key business ingredients—finance, economics, marketing, management, and accounting—which I thought necessary to be more effective in my job. As a result, I am of the opinion that an M.B.A. is an excellent degree for enhancing one's background, especially for those with a liberal arts education. However, I strongly believe that business school is more meaningful and relevant to those who have had prior work experience, as there exists a context in which to augment the course of study.

Upon completion of my M.B.A. in February 1979 I entered the bank's commercial credit training program in order to be a part of the bank's basic business—lending—and to round out my banking experience. I was assigned to the district specializing in the garment/textile/entertainment industries. Handling a portfolio of small business and middle market customers was a challenge. I analyzed and determined credit needs, structured deals and provided cash management servicing.

Late in 1980 I was asked to join the division's strategic planning unit, which was then undergoing expansion. After a little more than a year as deputy department head, I was promoted to director of the unit, which is my current position. Planning has become increasingly important due to the deregulation of the banking industry. "What do we do now? Where do we want to be in five years? What new products/services should we offer?" These are just some of the challenges facing us as we anticipate the changes in banking law and the movements of our competition. In view of this changing environment created by deregulation, I began working toward a law degree to further supplement my background and experience.

Banking is experiencing tremendous growth and change—it's a whole new ballgame—evolving into a fully integrated financial services industry. The competition not only includes banking institutions, but has expanded to comprise brokerage and investment houses, retailers, high-tech companies, conglomerates, and so forth. As a result, those individuals seeking to enter the industry will need to be sales-oriented and well-rounded in financial services. Banking, finance, and credit will provide the basis, but securities, insurance, and other financial services will play key parts in the banking financial supermarket.

Judy Thompson, Age 33
Vice President
Continental Bank, Chicago, IL

I went to Iowa State University and majored in distributed studies, a curriculum I arranged with three areas of concentration in industrial administration, economics, and industrial engineering. My engineering studies emphasized capital budgeting and financial project management. When I graduated I looked for a job, and got tired of people asking me if I could type—which I couldn't. While I was in college I had spent some time in Japan doing a research project on the role of women in Japanese business, and I had become quite intrigued with the country. After four or five months of looking, when I really couldn't find the kind of job that I thought I should have, I made some contacts with people I had met in Japan and got a job teaching English, and picked up and went back. I stayed there for about a year and a half, and during that time I ended up working for a couple of small trading companies doing mostly English correspondence, but I had a lot of time to talk to the people and find out what their business was like. I was always interested in business, and I had every intention of eventually going and getting an M.B.A. But I knew I didn't want to do it right out of college, because what do you have to contribute, except what you learned in a book?

While I was overseas I did all my applications for business schools, and I came back to go directly to Harvard. When I was looking for a business school I knew that, having a technical undergraduate background, I wanted something a little less technical with more emphasis on communications. By the time I got to Harvard I knew I was interested in international business. I probably would not have chosen that coming right out of undergraduate school. I also knew that finance was my strongest suit, and I tailored my curriculum to that.

During the summer between my first and second year, I went to work for Continental as an intern in their European division, primarily to see if I liked international banking. It's an easy way to test a new career and one I'd recommend for everybody. During my second year I interviewed exclusively with banks because I wanted to go back overseas as rapidly as possible and felt that banking was probably the easiest way to do that. In hindsight though, I think it would have been better to have a wider choice of options and then narrow the field. In the end I went back to Continental because I liked the atmosphere, but I also felt that, having worked in the European division over the summer, I could probably get an overseas assignment relatively quickly. As it turned out that was not the case due to a worldwide reorganization and the creation of Continental's multinational banking department. With all the moving around of people, Europe was pretty much closed off; at that time only our branches there were large enough to take people who didn't have too much experience. And the way the Asia group was run you typically had to spend a couple of years in Chicago before you went overseas. So that's what I did. I spent two years being the liaison primarily for Taiwan, but also for Hong Kong and Korea, and then was transferred to Taipei.

In Taiwan for the first two years I was an account officer. Most M.B.A.s coming out of school and joining the lending side of a major bank would be account officers. An officer is assigned anywhere from ten to forty accounts, depending on the size of the accounts and the kind of business you do. At Continental an account officer has responsibility for marketing and for credit recommendations and credit structuring. So on any given day you may go out and make several calls on your customers or on prospects to become acquainted with the kinds of business they do, to see what kinds of services—be it money lending, cash management, or trust business—you can sell them. In Taiwan that meant mostly trade finance, letters of credit, and other documentary business, that is, processing documents for imports and exports. Like most countries, Taiwan has relatively complicated investment and financing laws and regulations and it was important to understand those fully in order to be able to advise customers. In fact, I think one of my more important roles was to act as a consultant to foreign companies doing business in Taiwan as to how best to structure and finance their companies—satisfying their own requirements yet staying with the local regulations.

I came back to the States about a year ago to be part of a newly created division which does an independent review and evaluation of all the risk assets of the bank. We look at every loan that is done within the bank and assign it a risk rating, based on the financial condition of the company, the industry, and so forth. We do both international and domestic transactions, but I've been working only on the domestic side. I cover about ten industry groupings, including cable television, forest products, and construction engineering.

There are a couple of things I really like about my present job. Because I have had a totally international background, being involved in domestic business is very interesting; the lending practices in the United States are in general much more sophisticated than they are in Taiwan. There are a lot of interesting financing structures that I've learned about in the last year, as well as legal aspects I'd never dealt with before. Also, being essentially an industry analyst is very challenging. That means looking in depth first of all at what we do: Are we comfortable with the level of risk we've got in a given industry? Why are we? I look at the characteristics of the industry, the companies, and the kinds of projects we lend to. It means delving into the industry itself. With this kind of job it's possible to act as a clearinghouse and a provider of information, which is a role I enjoy.

There's an opportunity to do a lot of facilitating in a field like banking. Most banks are structured so that you can be a generalist or you can become an industry specialist. Even as a generalist you get to know certain industries well. For example, in Taiwan I ended up doing a lot of lending to the petrochemical industry, and became a source for people in Asia. It's important to use your knowledge and experience to develop unique skills—which can be used in the bank or on the outside, for that matter.

THE ELECTRONICS INDUSTRY

E NTREPRENEURIAL success stories abound about high-tech companies that literally began in a garage less than a decade ago and have now quickly become million-dollar businesses. Longer established companies, their recent growth fueled by the advent of the transistor in 1948 and the ensuing development of integrated circuits and the silicon chip, are neighbors and competitors of these high-tech startups. Their common business is the development, production, and sale of electronic components and the electronic systems they are used in.

Technological advancements are always right around the corner in this industry—if they're not happening already. Today more reliable components, such as smaller, denser chips with greater memory capacity, are being developed. Even as an improved design hits the market a better one is in the works. With this business climate, a microcomputer with 64K (8000-bit) memory capacity can become obsolete as soon as a competitor releases one with a memory twice as large.

This constantly changing picture makes for an industry in serious internal competition, a situation that companies are handling in a variety of ways. One key survival strategy for many companies is to tailor their products for a specific market. Computer manufacturers, for instance, are aiming at distinct customer niches rather than information-processing users in general. They design their products especially for the use of hotels, athletic leagues, industrial process control users, or some other specialized application. Others are choosing to meet the competition head-on, by keeping up with the technology and releasing products that are ahead of the competition's. Or they copy the competitor: The current wave of "plug-compatible" machines in home computers and home media centers is a case in point.

The unique appeal for M.B.A. graduates is in the many opportunities to work at the very heart of a technology that's in constant progression and change and in a business that reflects this vitality. Many companies have vigorous marketing departments and look for candidates with graduate school experience in that area. Sound analytical capabilities and an understanding of the use of quantitative methods in a business environment are essential if you have your M.B.A. and want to work in the finance division of the company. Production management, or manufacturing, is a position that requires excellent interpersonal and supervisory skills.

Many firms prefer job candidates who have a technical undergraduate background in engineering, math, or computer science in addition to the M.B.A., because as the technology grows increasingly complex, technical ability becomes more important in every area of the company's operations. Previous work experience in the field or a demonstrated interest in the technology is also helpful.

Job Outlook

Job Openings will Grow: As fast as average

Competition for Jobs: Keen

At the larger computer and electronics companies, competition is especially fierce for nontechnical M.B.A.s because there is a larger pool of them from which to choose.

New Job Opportunities: Startup and expansion bring concomitant job opportunities, and the industry is continuing to grow. According to a study conducted by the University of Santa Clara, since 1978 more than 1000 companies have been formed just in Silicon Valley, California's stretch of high-technology businesses. Several well-known companies create new, self-contained divisions when existing ones edge up to 2000 employees. The number of these new divisions is increasing yearly, bringing new job openings along the way.

Marketing is an especially promising area for M.B.A.s. As computer applications expand in consumer, commercial, and industrial areas, many companies are placing renewed emphasis on marketing efforts. They are aware of the necessity of understanding customers' changing needs so that they may develop equipment to meet those needs and set up marketing and distribution channels to bring their product to the consumer.

Geographic Job Index

Since the industry's inception, the dominant areas for computers and electronics companies have been California's Silicon Valley and Route 128 outside Boston. These locations were determined in part by the engineering talent coming out of Stanford University and the Massachusetts Institute of Technology. Generally speaking, Silicon Valley has a greater number of components companies, while Route 128's concentration is in manufacturing the computers and systems that use these components. In the mid-seventies, nearly 80 percent of electronics companies were located in one or the other of these high-tech areas. Now, however, high-tech has begun to spread out. Texas, Florida, Pennsylvania, Colorado, North Carolina, New York, and Minnesota are becoming major locations for the industry. Many companies that may have originated in California or Massachusetts now have divisions in areas across the country.

Who the Employers Are

ELECTRONIC COMPONENTS MANUFACTURERS provide the parts from which computers and other electronic systems are built: integrated circuits and semiconductors ("computers-on-a-chip"), transistors, capacitors, resistors, switching devices, and others.

ELECTRONIC SYSTEMS AND EQUIPMENT MANUFACTURERS design, produce, and market a variety of products to meet commercial, consumer, scientific, industrial, and military needs. Companies may serve one or more of these markets, but in general the industry may be broken down into the following product segments:

> Computers: a range of products from large mainframe computers to minicomputers to desktop models; peripheral hardware (memory systems, disc drives, line printers, terminals)

> Office Machines: word processors, electronic typewriters, photocopiers, calculators

> Consumer Products: video cassette recorders and players, video games, radio and television receivers, stereophonic sound systems, personal calculators, microwave ovens, and electronic automotive accessories (such as pollution control devices)

> Industrial Control and Processing Equipment: factory automation devices and instruments for the measurement and control of manufacturing process variables such as flow rate and temperature

Communications Systems: computerized telephone systems; fiber optics systems, which conduct light along a tube for a variety of scientific and industrial uses

Medical Electronic Products: automatic blood pressure analyzers, ultrasound scanners, pacemakers, patient monitors

Military Systems: equipment for aerospace operations and communications, radar defense, air traffic control, missile control

Major Employers

ELECTRONIC COMPONENTS
Advanced Micro Devices, Sunnyvale, CA
General Instruments, New York, NY
Gould, Inc., Rolling Meadows, IL
Intel, Santa Clara, CA
Motorola, Schaumburg, IL
National Semiconductor, Santa Clara, CA
Raytheon Company, Lexington, MA

ELECTRONIC SYSTEMS AND EQUIPMENT
Apple Computer, Cupertino, CA
Burroughs Corporation, Detroit, MI
Control Data, Minneapolis, MN
Data General, Westwood, MA
Digital Equipment Corporation, Maynard, MA
General Electric Company, Fairfield, CT
Hewlett-Packard Company, Palo Alto, CA
IBM Corporation, Armonk, NY
NCR Corporation, Dayton, OH

Perkin-Elmer, Oceanport, NJ
ROLM, Santa Clara, CA
Sperry Corporation, New York, NY
Tandy Corporation, Fort Worth, TX
Texas Instruments, Inc., Dallas, TX
United Technologies Corporation, Hartford, CT
Wang Laboratories, Inc., Lowell, MA
Westinghouse Electric Company, Pittsburgh, PA
Xerox, Stamford, CT

How to Break into the Field

It helps if you have an engineering or computer science background. Although not all companies are strict about requiring technical experience, many recruiters for the larger firms use this requirement as one way to sift through the large number of M.B.A. applicants. Smaller companies look for this technical ability because they lack the resources for training and therefore prefer people who are familiar with the technology and can come up to speed very quickly once they're hired.

This doesn't mean that all high-tech doors are closed to M.B.A.s who were liberal arts majors as undergraduates. A finance or marketing concentration, rather than a general business school program, gives you an advantage. You should also demonstrate an interest in and familiarity with the industry and its products and technology. Trade journals and even newspapers and newsmagazines can help you get this information. Focus on one or two segments of the industry, rather than trying to take it all in. If office systems interests you more than aerospace, for instance, collect information on the companies that market word processors rather than those that make surveillance systems.

Some companies have established training programs. M.B.A.s might be hired for a marketing, finance, or manufacturing training program, for example, or a more broad-based program that provides exposure to many different areas of this firm. Upon completing the program, the trainee might then interview for positions throughout the company.

Many high-tech companies are actively recruiting M.B.A.s on campus. If your school's placement office is no longer an available resource for you, you will have to introduce yourself by letter. Call the companies you're interested in to find out which personnel representative handles M.B.A. recruiting or hires for the division you're interested in. Send your résumé with a cover letter highlighting your qualifications and expressing your interest in working with the company. You will probably receive a reply within two weeks, but following up with a phone call can't hurt and very definitely helps to emphasize your interest.

Don't hesitate to use contacts. Companies receive a lot of unsolicited résumés, so any personal or alumni contacts that can help to get you on the inside for an interview are valuable.

Although newspaper help-wanted ads may seem heavily directed toward programmers or engineers, careful combing can uncover opportunities for M.B.A. graduates. You may also want to register with those personnel agencies that specialize in placing people in the high-tech industry.

You can't be too persistent. Although some companies—especially young, rapidly growing firms—can be vague and hard to pin down about job opportunities, don't let that keep you from trying. Many companies believe this is a good screening tool in itself—that those who are persistent and keep pushing for the interview are most likely to succeed in their fast-paced environment.

International Job Opportunities

Many computer and electronics firms have large foreign operations, but opportunities in those divisions for U.S. citizens are extremely limited. Overseas openings are generally filled by people of that particular country.

MARKETING

It used to be that high-tech companies devoted enormous energy to the technical superiority of their products and paid very little attention to the customer who might be buying the products. However, in many segments of the industry—especially computers—this attitude is changing. As computers become more of an everyday commodity, companies are realizing that you can no longer get by on the strength of your product alone. You have to have marketing strategies that will increase your penetration of the marketplace.

Although companies will vary in their organizational structure, a product marketing group will in general be responsible for two functions: overseeing the planning of future products and the broad-based long-range marketing strategy, and coordinating the various activities required to get a new product to market.

With an M.B.A., your first job in marketing might be as a product manager. You would be responsible for one product and all the marketing activities related to it—from establishing the most profitable price to handling promotion. The stage the product is in when you arrive will determine what your first duties will be. If the company is just introducing it, you'll probably spend your first few weeks writing sales documents and training manuals. If it's in the development stage and won't be introduced for two years, you might start off doing market surveys or working with the engineers on establishing certain special features and charting production schedules.

Sometimes an M.B.A. might get experience on the sales force before entering marketing. This can be a valuable path to follow, because the experience of being out in the field gives you a better feel for what the customers need and what's going to work in terms of marketing strategies.

Qualifications

Personal: Creativity. Enterprise. Energy. High commitment to the job. Ability to work well with others.

Professional: Excellent analytical skills. Ability to communicate in writing.

Career Paths

LEVEL	JOB TITLE	EXPERIENCE NEEDED
Entry	Product manager	M.B.A.
2	Product line manager	3-5 years
3	Product marketing manager	5-10 years
4	Marketing manager	10+ years

Job Responsibilities

Entry Level

THE BASICS: Analyzing customer market surveys. Obtaining literature about the competition and studying it. Helping write sales training manuals and sales aids.

MORE CHALLENGING DUTIES: More responsibility in all aspects of product planning—introduction, pricing, promotion, sales training. Studying new market opportunities.

Moving Up

If you show administrative ability, your next step could be into the position of product line manager. You'd be responsible for an entire line of products and the product managers who handle each individual product of that line. (A company may have several product line managers, each responsible for a different line.) With your broader viewpoint, you'll assist the product managers, approve their marketing plans, answer questions, and help solve problems. In general, you make and approve final decisions for the whole product line.

Your success and the success of your product line could put you into the job of product marketing manager. Product line managers will report to you, and you'll also be responsible for longer-range planning, figuring out what new products the company needs—taking into account any technical advances on the horizon, what customers are asking for, and what market areas haven't yet been covered.

The marketing manager oversees the whole product marketing group from product managers to line managers to product marketing manager. Depending on the structure and size of the company, the marketing manager might also be responsible for other groups such as sales support, service or customer order processing.

FINANCE

As a member of the financial staff, you are part of a business advisory team, one that provides assistance to all corners of the company's management in making final decisions.

The financial staff analyzes and interprets financial data pertaining to a decision and makes recommendations based on their evaluation. For instance, if the production manager has determined that they need a new machine on the factory floor, the decision to purchase the machine and the planning of funds to finance the expenditure would be guided by the financial staff.

In general, the financial function in a computer and electronics firm may be broken down as follows.

FINANCING AND INVESTMENT: Overseeing the company's cash and other liquid assets; raising funds in the capital markets; investigating funds in various projects.

FORECASTING AND LONG-RUN PLANNING: Projecting costs, changes in technology, funds needed for investment, product demand. Using forecasts and other statistics to plan future operations.

PRICING: Determining profit levels for various price structures.

Because of the rapid growth of the electronics industry, as well as the rapidly changing technology, high-tech companies are facing tremendous challenges in the area of finance. Decisions to buy new equipment, build another manufacturing facility, or start another sales office must be faced almost daily. And these very necessary projects need long-range planning for financial support.

Qualifications

Personal: Leadership ability. Ability to work well with a team. A commitment to excellence. An appreciation of detail.

Professional: High academic achievement. Sound analytical capabilities. Good knowledge of finance and accounting principles. Effective communications skills.

Career Paths

LEVEL	JOB TITLE	EXPERIENCE NEEDED
Entry	Financial analyst	M.B.A.
2	Group manager, department manager	2-4 years
3	Director of finance, treasurer	4-8 years
4	Vice-president	8-10 years

Job Responsibilities

Entry Level

THE BASICS: Researching and learning the company's business and its operations, products, and markets. Providing a variety of miscellaneous data relating to budgets, short-term forecasting, capital equipment justifications, and monthly performance review.

MORE CHALLENGING DUTIES: Helping to analyze, interpret, and make recommendations based on financial data. Preparing reports for department manager. Conducting profitability studies on special projects, new market proposals, pricing recommendations, acquisition studies.

Moving Up

Keeping on top of the workload and successfully mastering the skills of the analyst can lead to a promotion to department manager. You may then oversee a group of analysts who handle the needs of a particular department (marketing, production, etc.), and you will work with managers from that department, presenting and discussing the recommendations that your group has come up with. You'll also participate in long-range forecasting and planning.

A promotion to director of finance would further broaden your supervisory realm. You might oversee the work of the financial managers for several departments. Depending on the company's size, the ladder may continue up several more rungs from vice-president and senior vice-president to executive vice-president and chief executive officer.

PRODUCTION MANAGEMENT

Manufacturing, or production, is the transformation of technology into real-life products. All the great ideas, marketing plans, and financial backing become relatively unimportant if the necessary components can't be turned into a saleable product or system—on schedule.

On a production line, you have components or parts, and the people and machines that assemble the parts. The operations management group makes sure you have the right parts and enough of them. It helps decide how many end products need to be configured from these part to fulfill promised delivery dates. Complex manufacturing companies, particularly in the electronics industry, face increasingly difficult operations management challenges. Their rapid growth, increasingly limited resources, and the complex technical environment make it difficult to make the most productive use of people, machines, budgets, and ideas.

The terms manufacturing, production, and operations are often used interchangeably, but they can be loosely defined as the actual assembly of products (production, manufacturing) and the support functions of the assembly—scheduling the assembly, purchasing the component parts that are assembled into the product, providing engineering services (operations). M.B.A. graduates might start in production as supervisors responsible for managing the assemblers or inventory personnel. As they are promoted, they take on more of the operational planning and support responsibilities.

Qualifications

Personal: Excellent interpersonal skills. Self-motivation. Organizational flexibility. Willingness to take risks. A realistic outlook.

Professional: Ability to organize and articulate ideas and concepts and communicate them clearly.

Career Paths

LEVEL	JOB TITLE	EXPERIENCE NEEDED
Entry	Production supervisor, Operations analyst	M.B.A.
2	Production manager	5 years
3	Director of operations, Plant manager	10 years

Job Responsibilities

Entry Level

THE BASICS: Analyzing material needs and purchasing. Product inventories. Forecasting.

MORE CHALLENGING DUTIES: Planning material purchasing for a production line. Coordinating production schedule using these materials. Making sure shipment orders are met. Supervising assemblers and employees keeping inventory records. Supervising product quality control testing.

Moving Up

The challenges faced by M.B.A.s in entry-level production jobs can be hard ones. Supervisory and interpersonal skills are put to a rigid test on the factory floor. The importance of details is brought home as scheduling and material requirements become real-life issues and not just problems on paper. As a production or operations manager, you will focus more on strategic and future goals. You might work with the marketing and sales division on sales projections and what that means in terms of actual hardware or parts needed for production. You may oversee several production lines and the work of the production supervisors.

ADDITIONAL INFORMATION

Salaries

Mean annual starting salaries of 1983 M.B.A.s: $24,000 to $40,000

In some cases, salaries may be considerably higher.

Working Conditions

Hours:　As a product manager, you may find yourself putting in overtime during the rush before a new product is introduced. Otherwise, you'll probably work 40 to 45-hour weeks.

Hours for a financial analyst are generally nine to five but, depending on your projects, you could find yourself putting in some late nights, especially at the end of the month or at year-end.

As a production supervisor, your work involves the factory workers, most of whom leave by five. So you're challenged not to put in long hours, but to get as much done as possible when your staff is on hand.

Environment:　At many computer companies, you'll probably find a very informal and relaxed atmosphere—open office doors, first names for everyone, ideas exchanged face-to-face instead by memo. So while the company in its entirety may be very large, the small company atmosphere is retained.

If you work in finance and marketing, you'll be in an office environment. In production, your office and the factory floor are likely to be the same, so you will be working in a noisy, peopled environment.

Workstyle:　As a product manager, most of your time will be spent at your desk preparing sales material and reading industry-related and product-related material. You'll also spend time on the phone or in meetings with engineers, sales reps, or customers.

The financial analyst spends the day at a desk, pencil behind the ear, calculator humming, or talking with people from other departments.

Production supervisors usually spend less time at their desks than they do at meetings, trouble-shooting on-line problems, and talking things over with other supervisors either by telephone or during a quick visit.

Travel: In customer marketing, you will probably make two trips per month, each lasting three to four days, to meet with customers. In product marketing, one four-to-five-day trip per month is average. In these trips you will be meeting with customers and sales reps and perhaps conducting training sessions for the sales force. There is virtually no travel for finance personnel at entry level, although in more senior positions you may visit other company sites once per quarter. In production, the amount of travel you do depends on the size of the company and the number of divisions. There is generally very little—other than a walk across the street to the main offices from the factory.

Internships

Some firms have regular summer programs for M.B.A.s; others hire on an as-needed basis. Contact the placement office on campus for information, or write directly to the college recruiter at firms that interest you.

Recommended Reading

BOOKS

The Computer Establishment by Katherine Fishman, Harper & Row: 1981

IBM: Colossus in Transition by Robert Sobel, Times Books: 1981

The Soul of a New Machine by Tracy Kidder, Little, Brown & Company: 1981

PERIODICALS

There are a large number of these, many of them excellent; the two below are particularly helpful.

Computer Decisions (monthly), 50 Essex Street, Rochelle Park, NJ 07662

High Technology (monthly), 645 Stewart Avenue, Garden City, NY 11553

Professional Associations

American Federation of Information Processing Societies
1899 Preston White Drive
Reston, VA 22091

Computer & Business Equipment Manufacturers
  Association
311 First Street N.W.,
Suite 500
Washington, DC 20001

Electronic Industries Association
2001 Eye Street, N.W.
Washington, DC 20006

Electronic Representatives Association
20 East Huron Avenue
Chicago, IL 60611

INTERVIEWS

Jean Barron, Age 30
Production Section Manager
Hewlett-Packard
Waltham, MA

When I graduated from Princeton in 1975 with a degree in art history, what I really wanted to do was follow my long-founded interest in children and adult education. I took a job as director of a children's museum in Savannah, GA, which wasn't far afield from my goal because it was applying education in a nonacademic setting. I really liked that, and I liked managing people.

I decided to go back to school for a master's degree in business administration from Harvard. I took a lot of managerial behavior courses, but I also fell in love with an introductory course on production and operations management, which I ended up concentrating in. I was thrilled to have discovered this aspect of a business. I thought it was fun and fulfilling to get your hands right in there on how products actually get made.

After business school, I joined Hewlett-Packard in their personnel department as manager of all their employee management training programs at their division in Waltham, MA. There were about 1500 employees there. I really think this was a perfect first job. When you join a company, it's important to get a feel very quickly for how the whole organization operates, and my job in personnel really allowed that. If I was going to direct the programs that train people throughout the company, I sure had to have an idea of how the whole thing worked!

Two and a half years later, I switched jobs within the company from personnel to production. Our factory makes medical electronic equipment—patient monitors, for example—for hospitals. I've been section manager for two different areas of production. Now I run a circuit board assembly group. My production line actually loads printed circuit boards with the components and circuitry that are required to make the products work. I manage five supervisors, who in turn have 65 assemblers reporting to them.

Basically there are two avenues of my background that have helped in my current job. One is the experience that I've had in managing people and teaching adults, because a lot of what I do now is to teach my five supervisors how to do their jobs well. So much of being a good manager in manufacturing is not only being innovative with the process that you introduce and manage, but also being effective through other people.

The other avenue that has helped tremendously is the work I did at business school in production and operations management—learning the scope of how a whole factory works.

People will say to me, "You work at Hewlett-Packard? But you're not an engineer." I think if you have some compensating strength that is valuable enough it can make up for not having a technical degree. I think in a middle-management job like mine (whether in manufacturing or in marketing here at Hewlett-Packard) there are three important requirements: technical expertise, analytical or business skills, and interpersonal skills. My interpersonal skills are always being honed by my occasional in-house training, and I'm always trying to keep my business analysis skills sharp—being able to see the forest for the trees, being able to analyze things in a clear way that presents objectives well, being able to run my production section like a small business.

The production floor and my office are one and the same. It's a very open environment. My desk is in the middle of the floor—I'm often surrounded by shelves of printed circuit boards—and from where I sit I can see my entire operation.

I think what's more fulfilling is meeting and achieving objectives through a team effort. And because my job is mostly people-interactive and verbal, I rarely take work home, which I like. I think it's important to keep work and play separate. But my days are long and full.

I love what I do. I know a lot of my business school classmates wouldn't like to be doing what I do. Consulting or staff positions higher up in a company are more popular than line jobs, even early in one's career. But I feel this career path not only has its rewards but also its potential.

Ray Sansouci, Age 32
Market Business Planner
Gould Electronics
Andover, MA

My first job after graduation from Dartmouth College was with Westinghouse Electric in a technical marketing assignment. Although I majored in engineering, I had decided that I didn't want to be a design engineer. This job in technical marketing was perfect—it allowed me to be on the business end of things and, at the same time, stay involved in technology.

A few years later I moved to Columbus, Ohio, and spent three and a half years as a field engineer with the Westinghouse Industrial Products group. I sold control equipment and electric motors to industrial accounts. While I was selling, I decided I wanted to learn more about business and I enrolled in the night school business program at Ohio State University. The pace of night school, a full time job and a family was too hectic for me, though, so I decided to take a leave of absence and go to school full-time. I entered the M.B.A. program at the Harvard Business School.

Two years later, after graduation, I was employed by Gould, Inc., Electronics Systems in the Programmable Controller Division. I began as a product marketing manager for I/O products and took over one of the Controller product lines about a year later. My responsibilities at Gould allowed me to do just about everything they said I would do when I took product marketing at business school. We did everything from interfacing with the engineering department as to what features to design into the products to creating sales aids and even producing and giving audio-visual presentations.

My most recent assignment is in business and strategic market planning. It involves broader, strategic-level analysis of the market rather than a specific product analysis. We look at questions like where we will be in a year or two from now, how the market is changing, what competitors are on the horizon, and what technologies are coming at us and how they will affect our business.

Like most high-tech companies, we have our share of problem areas such as missed schedules or not having all the products we could use to back up our market position. However it seems most everyone in these industries has similar problems. When you're designing products on the forefront of technology as we are, things don't always go as planned.

Working in marketing at Westinghouse was different. The product line that I was involved with was more "old-tech" than high-tech. Things moved much more slowly there. For instance, there was a major new product announcement in 1969, and when I got there in 1974 it was still considered big news in my division.

The exciting part about working here at Gould is being a part of so much change. I mean, if you're not planning and developing products for introduction two years from now, you're already behind your competitors. The daily demands are intense, but it's exciting and worth it.

I think factory automation is one of the most dynamic sectors of the electronics industry. I came into this business because I thought that if the United States was going to come out of the recession (this was in 1982) and once again become a competitive producer of manufactured goods worldwide, it would have to start in our factories. Increasing productivity through factory automation would be one of the things that will help turn industry around.

THE ENERGY
INDUSTRY

IN the early 1970s Americans were suddenly shaken out of the complacent belief that the fuel on which we depend so heavily was in unlimited supply. There were lines of automobiles at gasoline pumps for the first time since World War II. Lowered thermostats and dimmed lights became not only economical but imperative. But inconveniences to the individual consumer reflected much more than that. For the first time the industrial and economic sectors of the country realized how deeply vulnerable manufacturing and commerce were to the whims of the oil sheiks.

Reacting to the OPEC embargo, industry and government were forced into a search for new oil reserves and new energy resources. Buoyed by a windfall of government funding aimed at underwriting the discovery, development, and refining of new reserves and the tapping of alternative technologies, the energy industry experienced a boom. Expansion meant increased hiring, and for the first time M.B.A.s were in demand in an industry that had never before been particularly receptive to business school graduates.

Caught by surprise in the energy crunch, the oil companies awoke to the need for better economic planning and forecasting, and to emphasize these in a way they had not in the past. Consumers, newly aware of the need to conserve fuel, were buying less; business was becoming more competitive. It has been estimated that today consumer consumption of oil is down 7 to 10 percent from what it was a decade ago, before the embargo. The new mood of aggressive competition has accelerated a trend toward hiring business school graduates trained to deal with the demands of an uncertain market.

Another trend that has led to a greater interest in hiring M.B.A.s within the industry is the diversification that many of the larger companies have turned to. The powerful "seven sisters," the group of multinational companies whose combined influence amounts to that of a nation-state, have branched out into a variety of different industries. These new interests include such areas as information technologies, the prospecting and mining of minerals, and the development of new chemicals.

One study estimated that in the ten years between 1975 and 1985 the capital and exploration funds needed by the energy industry will exceed $900 billion, more than three times what was needed in the previous ten-year period. This flurry of activity—the new exploration and development projects, the diversification moves— is helping to increase the demand for business school graduates skilled in business analysis, forecasting, and management.

Another trend that has distinguished the energy industry in the last decade, and that has had its effect on job hopefuls, is the development of a whole panoply of clean and renewable energy alternatives. As we see our conventional energy resources dwindle early into the next century, the search for these will increase in importance.

Solar energy, the leading contender in this alternative energy effort, is still at an early stage in its development. A fluid and fledgling field, more of a cottage industry, there are some 5000 companies creating, selling, and distributing solar technology equipment, most of these small, grass-roots, entrepreneurial firms. Only a handful—probably fewer than 50—of these companies employ more than 30 people.

Job Outlook

Job Openings Will Grow: More slowly than average

Competition for Jobs: Keen

Today the energy industry is in a holding pattern. It is an industry very much influenced by political crosscurrents, and right now the flow of government funding has been dramatically curtailed. Meanwhile, energy consumption is down, in large part the result of rising fuel costs and growing conservation efforts among the general public. Above all, the industry was hit late but hard by the recent recession, and this has forced most of the companies in the field to reduce their hiring to a trickle.

There is tough competition for the few slots open. A recent study of the major oil companies by the Association of M.B.A. Executives found that major companies interview many more M.B.A.s than they have openings for. For example, Exxon will normally winnow through approximately 3000 M.B.A. hopefuls to fill an estimated 150 to 175 openings. Standard Oil of California, with a total work force of 41,000, normally interviews some 600 M.B.A.s every year before hiring between 20 and 30 of these candidates. The study also revealed that Atlantic Richfield hires some 20 to 25 M.B.A.s out of the 1000 that they interview annually. Gulf Oil interviews 300 but ends up hiring somewhere between 25 to 30 M.B.A.s every year, out of a total work force of 35,000.

New Job Opportunities: Once solar energy and other renewable forms of energy begin to be adopted by more businesses, communities, and individuals, job opportunities will increase. One congressional study predicted that 2.2 million jobs in renewables and conservation would be created by the year 2000. A promising sign in this area is that many of the energy industry giants have begun investing in alternative energy development programs with an eye to the future. Meanwhile, the continuing diversification of the industry, along with the expansion of smaller and medium-size oil and gas companies, most of them based in Oklahoma and Texas, are harbingers of a brighter job future. Recent scientific studies indicate that there could well be reserves of natural gas in places where it was once thought that natural gas could not collect. New exploration and extraction projects could result from these findings in coming years, offering expanded opportunities in the planning and management of these projects. Insiders also feel that once the industry comes out of the trough of the recession it will begin throwing the doors open to new employees in a way reminiscent of the boom years of the late 1970s. M.B.A.s should be near the front of the hiring line when this happens.

Geographic Job Index

The prestigious multinationals are headquartered in major metropolitan areas, such as Los Angeles, CA, Houston, TX, San Francisco, CA, Dallas, TX, and New York, NY. The smaller and medium-size independents, which provide almost half of the nation's oil and gas, are based in various parts of the country, although most of them are headquartered in Texas and Oklahoma. The petroleum services and equipment companies are also concentrated in the Southwest, as are the banks that cater to this industry. Energy investment banking firms are located all over the country, primarily in large cities. It should be noted that even though the big companies—the top 30 or so energy companies— are headquartered in big cities, an entry-level job in one of these companies may involve working in a smaller, regional office.

Who the Employers Are

MULTINATIONAL FIRMS, including the glamorous seven sisters, refine and distribute most of the oil produced in the Middle East. They also have plants and diversified industries throughout the country.

INDEPENDENT COMPANIES are leaner versions of the multi-nationals. They are beginning to come out from under the shadow of the major oil and gas titans, and are taking up some of the slack now that hiring has tapered off in the large companies.

BANKS, particularly in Texas and Oklahoma, that specialize in handling the accounts of oil and gas companies, hire M.B.A.s to service those accounts. Increasingly they are looking for candidates with a technical background for these positions.

INVESTMENT BANKING FIRMS help underwrite the aggressive mergers and acquisitions and the far-flung diversification projects that now characterize this capital-intensive industry.

ALTERNATIVE ENERGY COMPANIES, though outside the main-stream today, may prove to be the standard bearers of the future.

Major Employers

MULTINATIONAL FIRMS
  Atlantic Richfield Company, Los Angeles, CA
  Exxon Corporation, New York, NY
  Gulf Oil Company, Pittsburgh, PA
  Mobil Oil Corporation, New York, NY
  Shell Oil Company, Houston, TX
  Standard Oil Company of California, San Francisco, CA
  Tenneco Oil Company, Houston, TX
  Texaco, White Plains, NY

INDEPENDENT COMPANIES
  Houston National Gas Corporation, Houston, TX
  Superior Oil Company, Indianapolis, IN
  Texas Oil and Gas Corporation, Dallas, TX
  Tosco Corporation, Los Angeles, CA

BANKS WITH ENERGY ACCOUNTS
Bank of the Southwest, Houston, TX
First National Bank and Trust Company, Oklahoma City, OK
Mercantile National Bank, Dallas, TX
Republic Bank, Dallas, TX

INVESTMENT BANKING FIRMS WITH ENERGY CLIENTS
Butcher & Singer, Philadelphia, PA
C.J. Lawrence & Company, New York, NY
Rauscher and Pierce Securities, Dallas, TX
Underwood-Neuhaus & Company, Dallas, TX

How to Break into the Field

Companies often prefer M.B.A.s with technical undergraduate backgrounds—engineering, geology, or geophysics—or prior business experience. Having the law of supply and demand heavily in their favor, they tend to hire graduates from the more elite business schools. Most of their recruiting is done directly on campus. Some companies will consult with teachers and heads of departments or will arrange to meet with top students in order to pick and choose from among the most desirable candidates. Personnel officers at these energy companies also suggest that job hopefuls seek assistance from the college placement officer about approaching an energy firm. They stress that those who want to break into the field be familiar with what is going on within the industry, and that before approaching a company, the applicant should know something about it—its organizational hierarchy, general policies, attitude toward innovation, and commitment to new technologies and to the environment. For candidates interested in working at one of the companies based in the Southwest, which is where the market really is, personnel managers admit that they are inclined to hire people from the area. The feeling is that a person with roots in the region will be more comfortable working there; they have found that transplanted easterners, or people from a big city, sometimes feel stifled working and living in a small Oklahoma or Texas town.

International Job Opportunities

Despite the image of the multinational oil titan with its far-flung empire of plants and refineries, there is not as much work overseas as one would imagine. Many companies, when they enter into an agreement with a foreign country to set up an overseas facility, agree to staff it with that country's nationals. Companies that market Saudi Arabian oil, like Texaco, Exxon, and Mobil, do have Americans in middle- and upper-management posts abroad. But what overseas postings there are come only after years of experience; they ordinarily do not go to employees new to the business.

MULTINATIONAL AND INDEPENDENT FIRMS

Each company in the energy industry has a definite structure of its own and a different organizational makeup. The most significant differences between the multinationals and the independents is job mobility—you can often move up faster in a smaller company.

In general most firms initiate recent M.B.A.s by assigning them to field operations for the first year or two. There they gain familiarity with the hands-on operation of the company and work closely with experienced engineers and managers. They may be part of a project team that is developing a new facility or exploration site, or work in a district office doing financial analysis, marketing, or planning. The next step may be a transfer back to headquarters or rotation to another field position, but with more responsibility.

M.B.A.s work principally in the areas of marketing and finance. In finance they may work in financial analysis, in the treasury department, or in the comptroller's office.

The marketing department is responsible for the positioning and distribution of the company's products in the marketplace. A marketing analyst might study methods of measuring consumer attitudes toward the company's products, review sales figures in order to evaluate product trends, or develop methods of improving product distribution channels. Typically, a marketing analyst for an oil company might be part of a team investigating how retail service stations might be more fully used, or analyzing th potential of a proposed new product. The M.B.A. might begin as a member of a team, with specific marketing area responsibilities, and then eventually become manager of a marketing group. Those in marketing are usually the visible representatives of the company, because they most often come into contact with dealers, suppliers, and the general public. Thus, middle and top management is often recruited through the marketing ranks.

Financial analysts conduct studies that help the company to make its important financial decisions. For example, when a company derives assets from a sale, a team of financial analysts embarks on an analysis of the best long-term and short-term investments for those assets. Should the money go into a new coal mine in Australia or into building two new, ocean-going tankers to transport crude oil? Financial analysts also make forecasts, calculating material and labor costs, and the impact of inflation on those costs, over the life of a project. Other duties include evaluating earnings reports, creating financial forecasts for operating units, making studies of the competition in the marketplace, and embarking on long-range studies that forecast the effects of new technologies and trends in the industry.

New financial analysts typically are rotated throughout the company in order to acquire a solid grounding in company organization and policies. They might spend a few years in a division office learning about operations in the field before working at corporate headquarters. First assignments are generally as part of a team. Moving up, a financial analyst might become head of a planning group, coordinating the activities of a division or group of divisions.

The treasury department manages the company's money. M.B.A.s in this department help to forecast and manage cash flow, oversee foreign exchange transactions, solicit sources of funding, and provide financial advisory services to the company and its subsidiaries and affiliates. An M.B.A. might negotiate and implement financial programs, design and administer cash management systems, and maintain relationships with banks and investment banking firms. As an assistant treasurer (usually the entry-level title), the M.B.A. would be part of a small team in the treasury department responsible for a specific division and reporting to the corporate treasury department.

The comptroller's office handles internal cash flow and bookkeeping for the organization. M.B.A.s with a background in accounting are hired to fulfill a wide range of accounting responsibilities. A recent M.B.A. might be part of an office in charge of keeping account of the assets, liabilities, and business transactions of the company. He or she might also help prepare budgets for and economic evaluations of projects or divisions. With more experience, an M.B.A. might take the initiative in establishing and maintaining internal accounting controls for the company. Those with an expertise in taxes might help put together a corporate leasing agreement or be part of a team analyzing the tax advantages or disadvantages of a diversification or acquisition.

Qualifications

Personal: Strong interpersonal skills. Ability to communicate, both orally and in writing. Flexibility.

Professional: Knowledge of business and finance. Skill with figures. Awareness of the influence of technological development. Interest in international economics and politics, United States energy policies, and environmental issues. Technical background helpful.

Career Paths

LEVEL	JOB TITLE	EXPERIENCE NEEDED
Entry	Assistant marketing or product manager Financial analyst Assistant treasurer or comptroller	M.B.A.
2	Manager in entry department	3 years
	Planner in division office	
3	Vice president	6-8 years

Job Responsibilities

Entry Level

THE BASICS: Learning the functions and procedures of your entry department. Becoming acquainted with the work and organization of the company as a whole.

MORE CHALLENGING DUTIES: Handling projects on your own, or leading a team project. Initiating and following through on projects.

Moving Up

There is no set pattern for advancement, and each company has its own policies. In some companies career advancement can come by moving up in one specific area within an operating company, gradually assuming line management responsibilities. In many other companies, however, M.B.A.s rotate among different departments and different sections of the company, so that by the time they assume a general line post they are familiar with the overall inner workings of the firm. (Typically, an M.B.A. at one of the major oil companies might spend two or three years in the comptroller's development program, then be transferred to a post as a financial analyst, perhaps a member of a team exploring the supply, marketing and planning policies of a particular technology.) Relocation is common during these early years, with moves coming every two to three years during the first ten to fifteen years of employment with the firm, usually culminating in line management responsibilities at corporate headquarters.

BANKING AND INVESTMENT BANKING FOR THE ENERGY INDUSTRY

Billions of dollars change hands as the energy industry does business, and banks and investment banking firms are on hand to serve the special financial needs of energy industry. Financial institutions are looking for candidates with a background suitable for serving those needs—employment in the field before graduate study, perhaps, or a technical undergraduate degree in geology, engineering or geophysics. The latter is becoming increasingly important. It is difficult for financial institutions to assess the viability of a proposed project without some knowledge of the advanced technologies involved.

The M.B.A. will generally begin work as a lending officer, assessing the credit worthiness of energy companies and their projects. He or she analyzes the firm's performance by consulting with its officers and by examining financial data. If a loan is not made the lending officer might suggest alternative sources of funding and keep an eye on the company in case its profit potential increases. A lending officer also monitors the industry, scouting out possible investments.

Once a decision is made to underwrite a company the account is assigned to a manager. He or she sees the loan through every step of the lending process, and keeps a close watch on the project. The account manager may provide other services such as arranging the financial setup for a complex joint venture partnership or helping the energy company put together other deals—drilling partnerships, for instance, or the acquisition of mineral rights to certain land areas.

Typically, the M.B.A. will spend his or her first year in a commercial lending program. This may be followed by three to five years' work as an account manager, which might lead to an assistant vice president post. In another five years he or she might become an associate vice president. Progress depends on the number and profitability of the deals an officer sponsors. Of course, titles and frequency of promotions vary widely among financial institutions.

ADDITIONAL INFORMATION

Salaries

Salaries depend greatly on academic qualification, the nature of the job and work experience. Starting salaries for entry-level M.B.A.s range anywhere from $28,000 to $34,000 a year. In a managerial position, after three years' experience, annual salaries are $40,000 and up; at vice presidential level the range is approximately $60,000 to $70,000 a year.

Working Conditions

Hours: Most professionals in the energy industry readily admit that they spend anywhere from 50 to 60 hours a week on the job. Normal duties take at least 40 hours per week and extra hours are spent reading work-related material, beating a deadline for a specific project or in meetings. Closing out the books for the year or putting out the annual report periodically calls for extra hours from those concerned.

Environment: Although corporate headquarters may be plush, the entry-level M.B.A. more often finds himself or herself in more modest division offices. In general you will be assigned a small office or private work space, but it will not be fancy. When out in the field, talking to engineers at refineries or chemists in laboratories, expect a casual, shirt-sleeves setting.

Workstyle: You will be spending a good deal of time at your desk studying project reports or in meetings presenting your analysis of them. Most of the work involves gathering and disseminating information both in the office and in the field.

Travel: The amount of time spent traveling depends on the company. Some companies say that business personnel travel rarely, perhaps 5 to 10 percent of the year, while a handful of the larger companies, with a network of affiliates and plants, note that their marketing and financial corps spend roughly a quarter of their time on the road.

Internships

A few companies do have intern programs, but they are not common in the industry, as some companies do not want to feel obligated to hire interns after they have been through the program. Standard Oil of Ohio is one exception, offering about 100 internships annually.

Recommended Reading

BOOKS

Careers in the Energy Industry by B. H. Kraft, Franklin Watts, Inc.: 1977

Energy Futures: Report of the Energy Project at the Harvard Business School, Robert Stobaugh and Daniel Yergin, eds., Random House: 1979

The Energy Job Finder by Mainstream Access, Inc., Prentice-Hall: 1981

Oil and World Power by Peter R. Odell, Penguin Books: 1979

The Seven Sisters by Anthony Sampson, Bantam Books: 1975

PERIODICALS

Hydrocarbon Processing (monthly), Gulf Publishing Company, Box 2608, Houston, TX 77001

Offshore (monthly), 1200 South Post Oak Road, Houston, TX 77056

Oil and Gas Journal (weekly), Petroleum Publishing Company, P. O. Box 1260, Tulsa, OK 74101

Petroleum Intelligence Weekly (weekly), 49 West 45th Street, New York, NY 10036

World Oil (monthly), Gulf Publishing Company, Box 2608, Houston, TX 77001

Professional Associations

American Petroleum Institute (API)
2101 L Street, N.W.
Washington, DC 20037

International Association of Energy Economists
John Hancock Tower
200 Clarendon Street
Boston, MA 02116

INTERVIEWS

Joanne Shore, Age 34
Senior Associate, Corporate Planning
Gulf Oil Corporation, Pittsburgh, PA

My background is a little different than that of most M.B.A.s working in the energy field. I was a science major in college, eventually graduating from Carnegie Mellon University with an M.S. in physics. After graduation, I went to work at Westinghouse where I was involved in research work dealing with nuclear reactors and their applications in energy. This experience, however, led me to realize that it was the business side of this industry that really appealed to me.

After four years at Westinghouse, I went back to school, to the University of Pittsburgh to get an M.B.A. I was recruited upon graduation by Gulf Oil, which is headquartered in Pittsburgh, to work in their corporate planning office. It is rather unusual for a recent M.B.A. to go directly into corporate planning, since planning generally involves familiarity with a company, its policies, products, organizational structure. Usually, you work a couple of years in other areas such as finance or marketing before you go into corporate planning.

In essence, there are three main functions within the planning group. We coordinate the planning process of the different divisions within the company, which might include setting timetables for the planning process or reviewing capital expenditure proposals that come through headquarters. We also function as the strategic arm in planning. Top management in this case comes to us to investigate a specific product, technology, or investment possibility. And we do a report. Finally, we do overall financial forecasting. This might include trying to anticipate how different political, economic, or industry trends might affect the company, or on a different level, we might study what an individual competitor or group is up to.

Planning is exciting because it involves analytical and conceptual talents. You have to be able to define a problem, think through a broad issue, and zero in on what is vital, or where, specifically, a problem lies. You have to be able to see overall patterns and pinpoint trends. Interestingly, I have found that my background in physics pays off, although not in any specific knowledge that I can bring, but rather in the kind of thinking that you develop when you study physics. The talent for conceptualizing, which lies at the core of the more advanced areas of physics, has provided me with an intellectual tool, a method of analysis.

Assignments vary greatly, and you work in teams. For example, I have worked with a planning group on a project studying the synthetic fuels industry and where it is going. This was certainly a challenging assignment, since the industry per se doesn't exist right now. So what we had to do was develop scenarios or models for this future activity.

It's all exciting to me because I work close to the decision makers in the company.

Joy Kendall, Age 32
Supervisor, Corporate Treasury
Mitchell Energy Corporation, Woodlands, TX

Originally I went into banking because I believed—and I really think that this is true—that banking is an excellent training ground for industry. I was recruited straight out of Louisiana State University (where I received my M.B.A.) by the Bank of the Southwest in Houston to work in their credit management program. It was a great first job, not only because it gave me a grounding in finance, but also because it brought me into contact with oil business executives. In fact, I came to Mitchell because of a connection made at the bank—an officer who later became the treasurer of Mitchell had worked with me there, and hired me to be the administrator of financial services.

In financial services, I was part of a team that helped develop investment packages, such as the financial arrangements for acquisitions, and create joint venture partnerships for the development of mineral interests. We also worked on the financing of current operations through different lines of credit.

From there I went to my present job, which involves a wide variety of responsibilities. In a typical day, I might study cash balances and receipts, or deal with the accounting department, or monitor the processing and disbursement of funds. The job requires that I deal with a lot of different departments and personnel—in management, accounting, data processing. Or I might talk with bank officers to find out whether they are providing us with the services that we might need.

Mitchell, like most big energy companies, has diversified interests. For example, the company has been in real estate since the 1960s. Because this is a capital-intensive business, you can have responsibility for handling millions of dollars. You have to be skilled in every area of finance, you have to be a good communicator who can get ideas across, and you should be open and receptive to changes and new ideas. One of the things I like about this company is that you are exposed to different things and learn about various sides of a complex, diverse, and changing field.

INVESTMENT BANKING

"OSGOOD is as much in love now as when we were first married," says the matron in the *New Yorker* cartoon, "but I discovered that, unfortunately, it's with investment banking."

That about says it, folks. A career in investment banking, if it is to be a successful one, is very much like a love affair, full of commitment, intensity, excitement, and reward. But like the marriage that follows, it is also filled with risk and requires an enormous amount of very hard work.

Competition for positions in investment banking is exceptionally keen, perhaps more so than in nearly any other field an M.B.A. might choose. The monetary rewards are very high and come sooner than in most other fields, but the pressure to perform, and to perform well, often better than your peers, is intense. Firms in the field are highly selective. Many of the available entry-level positions are filled automatically by the top students at the "upper tier" business schools. Because the stakes are so high, firms cannot afford to have anyone who is not extremely capable risking the vast amounts of capital that investment bankers handle as a matter of course.

Corporate underwriting, that is, raising capital by guaranteeing the sale of the issuing firm's or client's securities, is still largely the traditional business of investment banking. But the industry has undergone some major changes in recent years, in response to both uncertain economic conditions and the demand from corporations for more financial services. Many firms now offer advisory services, for example. However, expansion and diversification of services has not necessarily meant expansion of personnel. Although the industry is in a growth period (revenues in the six-year period between 1974 and 1980 more than tripled and are still rising), many firms continue to hire a very limited number of M.B.A.s in entry-level positions.

Because of this broadening of the field, it is important for those entering a firm to keep abreast of activities in all departments. If, as you are being exposed to the firm's business, you don't move naturally from one functional area to another, make an effort to do so on your own. With a knowledge of the different services and products the firm offers, future opportunities won't be limited. The more you understand about the firm's range of business and its style, the more you will be able to branch out and assume greater responsibility. This is not only expected of you, but demanded.

In return, incentive compensation packages are excellent and the monetary rewards will increase on an ongoing basis. But you will be expected to earn these rewards by being a self-starter, ambitious, highly motivated, energetic, and creative about going after business as well as coming up with innovative solutions to clients' financial needs. This entrepreneurial spirit must be combined with an ability to work on a team, often comprising upper-echelon firm members as well as corporate officers and upper-level managers from client firms. Considerable interpersonal and communications skills are essential, because you will also find yourself conferring with a variety of specialists from other fields—lawyers, accountants, bankers.

Investment banking is a high-powered, glamorous field. The atmosphere surrounding it is clublike and tends to be self-limiting. Those who enter it are successful if they meet the challenge of its fast pace and competitive atmosphere head-on. Billions of dollars and carefully cultivated reputations are at stake. A piece of this action can be had only with the sacrifice of personal time and private life that the field demands.

Job Outlook

Job Openings Will Grow: As fast as average

Competition for Jobs: Keen
Although there is growth in the industry, it is in the variety of services provided to clients. The number of M.B.A.s taken on to help perform these new functions has remained relatively constant because of the highly selective hiring standards that prevail.

New Job Opportunities: The investment banking industry is a cyclical one, sensitive to the economic climate of the country and the activity of the stock market and financial world in general. If the economy is growing, the volume of underwriting grows, and investment banking grows with it. Many functions that look like "new" areas are really only new ways of underwriting. Although they may have new names and sound more intriguing, they are still largely rooted in the major functional areas such as corporate and municipal finance.

There are no "hot" areas of investment banking, per se. It is not a business that lends itself to trendy thinking. However, two areas— mergers and acquisitions and trading and distribution—look as though they might offer greater opportunities for the M.B.A. in the future. Also, the proliferation of electronic equipment for business and personal use is spawning many new, smaller companies that have solid potential for success, though at greater risk. The trend does not show any signs of abating and may offer greater opportunities as these companies look for capitalization.

MERGERS AND ACQUISITIONS: M&A is a relatively new activity that is fast becoming a major area within the investment banking field. In response to a tight economy, companies are seeking to diversify as well as to expand, finding it cheaper to buy into an existing concern than to develop their own assets. Negotiating with firms can be very delicate, and work in this area requires considerable interpersonal and communications skills.

TRADING AND DISTRIBUTION, called sales and trading in some firms, now calls for a more sophisticated sales force, because the character of the business has changed so much. Consequently, investment banking firms are taking a more active role in the actual distribution to the public (mainly to institutions such as insurance companies, unions, etc.) of the securities they have underwritten. Increasingly, this is a means of entry into an investment banking firm, since some firms that hire sales associates give them the same exposure to other areas—corporate and public finance, for example—that they give any other new associates.

Geographic Job Index

New York, NY, the acknowledged financial capital of the world, has the widest opportunities in the investment banking field. All major investment banking firms, as well as national full financial service firms (which offer brokerage as well as investment facilities), have their main offices in New York, many of them in the Wall Street area.

However, regional opportunities are developing quickly. Many of the larger firms with branch offices in major cities throughout the country have enlarged their investment banking activity in these locations. Several firms are now handling only regional clients. Regionally based firms have the advantage of more direct access to potential clients and perhaps a better understanding of their needs as they relate to their locale and industry. Even with a more limited pool of possibilities and smaller bases of capital, these firms are gaining strength and may offer good opportunities for M.B.A.s to gain entry into the field. It is especially worth investigating if you have gained expertise in an area a regional firm may need. These firms sometimes send recruiters to campuses.

Personnel needs vary from firm to firm, but on the average, only 10 to 30 M.B.A.s make their way into the investment banking area in each firm, both the pure banking firms and the full financial service firms. This is a relatively small number when compared with the hiring practices in many other industries.

Who the Employers Are

Major Employers

Major employers are the largest investment banking firms and the high-profile Wall Street brokerage firms, all of which have investment banking divisions. These are often referred to as full financial service firms.

INVESTMENT BANKING FIRMS

Bear Stearns & Company, New York, NY
Dillon, Read & Company, New York, NY
The First Boston Corporation, New York, NY
Goldman Sachs, New York, NY
Kidder Peabody Company, Inc., New York, NY
Lazard Frères & Company, New York, NY
Morgan Stanley & Company, New York, NY
Salomon Brothers, New York, NY
Wertheim & Company, New York, NY

FULL FINANCIAL SERVICE BROKERAGE FIRMS

Bach Halsey Stuart Shields, Inc., New York, NY
Dean Witter Reynolds, Inc., New York, NY
E.F. Hutton Company, New York, NY
Merrill Lynch Pierce Fenner & Smith, Inc., New York, NY
Paine Webber, New York, NY
Shearson Lehman/American Express, Inc., New York, NY
Smith Barney Harris Upham & Company, Inc., New York, NY

There are other, smaller New York based investment banking firms which hire fewer M.B.A.s. You can contact these firms directly if they do not recruit on campus.

Regional Employers

INVESTMENT BANKING
Dain, Bosworth, Inc., Minneapolis, MN
The Inter-Regional Financial Group, Minneapolis, MN
Rauscher Pierce Refsnes, Inc., Dallas TX

FINANCIAL SERVICE BROKERAGE FIRMS
A.G. Becker, Inc., Chicago IL
Jaffray, Hopwood, Inc., Minneapolis, MN
Rotan Mosle, Houston, TX, now a subsidiary of Paine
    Webber, Inc., but maintaining their Houston office,
    among other locations

How to Break into the Field

Because of the variety of new opportunities—new areas of specialization and ways of capitalizing businesses—it is important to find out what the various firms are involved in and then to determine where your own interests lie. In general, business school placement services can supply the information you need: written materials describing the field and specific firms, packets that include recent articles, and statistics culled from various sources; some schools even offer videotapes. Make full use of such resources as the *Business Periodicals Index* and the *F&S Index of Corporations,* company brochures, and annual reports.

Many firms hire summer associates, or interns, who are between their first and second years of business school. This is one of the best avenues into the field. Those who demonstrate an aptitude for the work as well as the other qualities that point to success are often offered a full associate's position when they finish their education. Many firms expect to fill their entry-level associate positions in this way.

However, work experience elsewhere, either before graduate school or during it, is always looked on favorably. Although a job in a client-oriented business is particularly helpful, firms are also looking for the qualities that come with work experience: maturity, knowledge of the "real world," well-defined goals, motivation, ambition, capacity for hard work.

In the investment banking field, more than in many others, firms are looking for a high level of intelligence and achievement. The better reputation your business school has, and the closer to the top of your class you are, the better your chances of entering an investment firm. For example, the investment banking arm of one of the nation's largest full financial service firms recruits actively at only seven business schools. This does not mean that you don't have a chance if you attend a different school, but it does mean that you are going to have to work harder—persistently and creatively—to land a job.

Get in touch with alumni who may have contacts with the firms that interest you, and join campus clubs, such as the finance club, to create a network of other contacts. When speakers come to the campus, approach them after their speeches. They may be able to help you get a foot in the door. And don't hesitate to contact firms directly.

If you are able to interest a firm in you, be prepared for a long interview process. After an initial on-campus interview with a recruiter, you could spend a full day at the firm, seeing as many as six different people, sometimes more. Part of what the firm is looking for is the ability to maintain a high level of performance under pressure and in a highly competitive environment, so there are often between three and ten more interviews, both personal and informational, before the process is complete.

Even though you—and the interviewer—know that you will learn the most on the job, you must show a solid knowledge of the field and the firm. Learn everything you can about it; show that you care about and understand it. This is a good habit to get into. Investment banking is both complex and constantly changing, and if you enter it, there will be no let-up in the need to adapt to that change and complexity.

Many investment banking firms and top-rated graduate business schools require work experience as a condition for employment or admission. If you have an admission letter to graduate school in hand, investment banking firms are often willing to hire you as an analyst or in other positions and give you on-the-job training.

Deferred admission to business school can work in two ways: The school can admit the student on the basis of an undergraduate record but defer the starting semester until the applicant has worked for a year or two, or a student who has been admitted can request a deferral for a variety of reasons—a job offer, for example, or the need to earn tuition money.

Programs for the pregraduate, which exist at many major firms, are finite, usually lasting two years. They are not intended to provide long-term career opportunities, but if the two years have been successful for everyone concerned, you can certainly expect to return to the firm after earning your M.B.A.—if that is how you want your career to proceed.

Positions are also open at investment banking firms for students right out of college who demonstrate qualities that the firm is looking for, even though they may lack a solid background in finance or economics. Liberal arts, history, and English majors are in programs at leading investment banking firms. But the expectation is that once the program is over, it will be necessary to earn an M.B.A. to go any farther in the field. These programs are valuable because they allow you to establish a relationship with an investment banking firm, provide valuable work experience, and make admission to a top graduate school more likely. The investment banking firm usually makes no commitment to rehire you, and the hiring process after business school will probably be the same as described above for prospective employees. In some cases, however, there may be an understanding that you will eventually return to the firm in an associate capacity.

For more specific information on deferred admissions, contact your placement office, admissions offices of business schools, and personnel officers of individual firms. Policies and programs differ widely from school to school and firm to firm.

International Job Opportunities

International travel may not come your way until you have spent a certain amount of time with a firm, but some evidence shows that this is a growth area for M.B.A.s as investment banking expands its worldwide interests. Not all firms, however, have the same commitment to the international marketplace.

When investigating firms with international job opportunities, look for several things: Do they have U.S. clients with overseas interests? If so, do they send staff abroad to serve these corporations? Do they have overseas branches or subsidiaries, and are these staffed only by foreign nationals? Is there an international department at home headquarters so that you can observe its operations? Find out also which functional areas are likely to have international involvement. For example, at the moment there is a great deal of foreign interest in the mergers and acquisitions area.

In recent years, foreign corporations have begun to use American capital markets to finance some of their business, making the field quite competitive. Some experience in international banking and fluency in a foreign language will be helpful in finding an assignment overseas.

THE WORK

Although each firm is organized differently, the major functional areas in investment banking are corporate finance, municipal (or public) finance, mergers and acquisitions, financial advisory service, and private placement. With few exceptions, entry-level associates begin as generalists and are exposed to each of these areas of specialization during their training. (Some smaller firms that deal only in one area may hire a few entry-level M.B.A.s, but these positions are quite rare.)

CORPORATE FINANCE is the department that helps the company raise capital for the client's purposes (expansion of operations, new projects) through the underwriting of equities, bonds, or commercial paper. The investment banking firm advises the client on the best way to go about selling these securities. In addition, the firm takes an active role in buying the stocks, bonds, or commercial paper and then distributing them in an underwriting. Sometimes firms work together on a project, underwriting the sale of securities as a group. This is an area within corporate finance in which you can develop expertise and later specialize.

Firms in any type of industry may seek capital, and some investment banking firms specialize in particular types of industry. You might find yourself becoming a specialist in an industry. Some of the most up-and-coming areas of specialization are high tech, energy, and real estate.

MUNICIPAL (OR PUBLIC) FINANCE is the department that raises capital and deals with financial needs of state and local governments. In essence, it functions in the same way as the corporate finance department, but with a different set of clients. Specific activities may be in the areas of transportation, housing, water supply and sewage systems, for example.

MERGERS AND ACQUISITIONS is a field about which a number of evocative terms are being thrown around these days—"Pac Man defense," "shark repellents," "white knights." The investment banking firm serves a company contemplating a merger or acquisition by conducting a detailed analysis of the company under consideration—not only of its financial status, but also of the current state of its management and operations. The investment banker advises the client company whether the proposed expansion would be a positive move. After a decision has been made, the investment banking firm might be asked to handle the logistics of the deal. Conversely, a firm fighting a takeover may seek the assistance of an investment banking firm in retaining its independence.

FINANCIAL ADVISORY SERVICE is provided when an investment banking firm is asked to do a thorough study and analysis of a division that a company is thinking of selling. The investment banking firm assesses the value of that section of a large corporation's business and advises accordingly.

PRIVATE PLACEMENT involves a situation in which the investment banking firm serves as a placement agent, rather than underwriting securities. For example, an institution may decide, after consultation with an investment banker, that it would be preferable to sell a $25-million promissory note rather than make a public offering. In such a case, the investment banking firm would find one or more large institutions that would then share in loaning the capital.

ADDITIONAL INFORMATION

Qualifications

Personal: Demonstrated intelligence. Maturity. Ability to function under pressure. Self-motivation and entrepreneurial spirit. Capacity to work successfully on a team. High energy level. Enthusiasm. Ability to combine seriousness of purpose with a sense of humor.

Professional: Strong analytical skills. Oral and written communications skills. Leadership capability. Facility for handling many projects simultaneously. Excellent understanding of the financial world and its working. Work experience preferred but not essential.

Career Paths

LEVEL	JOB TITLE	EXPERIENCE NEEDED
Entry	Associate	M.B.A.
2	Vice president	4-6 years
3	Managing director or senior vice president	7-9 years
4	Partner	11+ years

Job Responsibilities

Entry Level

THE BASICS: Orientation/training programs in all aspects of the business, combining classroom and intensive on-the-job training. Preparing industry studies, prospectus drafts, and general research. Doing financial analyses.

MORE CHALLENGING DUTIES: Assignment to specific projects as part of a team that includes senior personnel. Specialization in a particular area.

Moving Up

This is a business in which it is important to learn fast and perform well soon—the faster and the sooner, the better for you and your career. As you move from associate to vice president, you spend more time in direct contact with clients. You will be expected to prepare financing proposals and presentations and to develop new business for the firm, proving your worth by increasing productivity and profits. Creativity plays a role— you are expected to solve clients' financial problems in innovative and sophisticated ways.

The managing director or partner oversees client relationships and, like the vice president, develops new business. Some also have management responsibility for running units and departments within the firm.

The job of top management is to direct the firm as a whole: defining the direction in which it should head and the best areas for expansion, initiating new concepts, investigating new financing opportunities, and overseeing employee management.

Salaries

Individual earnings result from a combination of base salary and incentive compensation (bonuses based on individual performance and the success of the firm). Total earnings of more than $100,000 a year are typical at the level of vice president. Incentive compensation becomes increasingly generous as you progress up the ladder, boosting a managing director's salary over $200,000 a year, with some earning much more.

Working Conditions

Hours: The hours are long and irregular. They depend a great deal on the market, and consequently tend to be cyclical—you may work a 50-hour week at one time and a 100-hour week at another. The time commitment expected of you is high, and many of those hours will be spent under pressure.

Environment: The environment is apt to be quite plush, because of the nature of the profession and the fact that many top-level executives visit the firm. Entry-level people are usually in some sort of cubicle; they need privacy for the concentration that their work demands.

Workstyle: The entry-level associate spends a great deal of time in front of a computer, working with the spread sheets that provide analytical data, and at the printer, checking prospectuses for accuracy. Tight deadlines and stressful situations are common. In many cases, work cannot be put off or rescheduled. However, there are also opportunities to meet with clients and to participate in the financing process—meetings that provide a chance to get out of the office and away from the computer terminal and the calculator.

Travel: Travel increases greatly as you move up in the firm, and there is also more travel at the entry level than in many other industries. Associates are often instrumental members of a team and travel to meetings along with upper-level personnel. Corporations are based throughout the country, so travel can be to almost any area of the United States.

Internships

Every major firm and many smaller ones have well-established summer internships or summer associate programs. These are normally for M.B.A.s who are between their first and second years of business school. Most firms are looking for the same qualities in their summer associates as they want to find in regular entry-level associates, so competition is keen and the process highly selective. The experience you gain, however, will be invaluable, because these positions offer solid exposure to the field and to the particular firm's approach. You will be part of a team and expected to do an associate's job from the start.

If you are interested in particular firms, contact them yourself as early as possible. Your placement office is a good resource for arranging interviews with companies that are sending recruiters to campus and for providing information on what firms offer internships and on application procedures.

Recommended Reading

BOOKS

Competition in the Investment Banking Industry by Samuel Hayes III et al., Harvard University Press: 1983

Investment Banking in America: A History by Vincent P. Caruso, Harvard University Press: 1970

Money on the Move: The Modern International Capital Market by M.S. Mendelsohn, McGraw-Hill, Inc.: 1980

PERIODICALS

American Banker (daily), 1 State Street Plaza, New York NY 10004

Barron's (weekly), 22 Cortlandt Street, New York, NY 10007

Bond Buyer (weekly), 1 State Street Plaza, New York, NY 10004

Financial World (biweekly), 1250 Broadway, New York, NY 10001

Forbes (weekly), 1221 Avenue of the Americas, New York, NY 10020

Fortune (biweekly), Time, Inc., 1270 Avenue of the Americas, New York, NY 10020

Institutional Investor (monthly), 488 Madison Avenue, New York, NY 10022

Institutional Investor (international edition, monthly), 488 Madison Avenue, New York, NY 10022

Journal of Portfolio Management (quarterly), 488 Madison Avenue, New York, NY 10022

Mergers and Acquisitions (quarterly), 229 South 18th Street, Rittenhouse Square, Philadelphia, PA 19103

Money (monthly), Time, Inc., 1270 Avenue of the Americas, New York, NY 10020

Venture (monthly), 35 West 45th Street, New York, NY 10036

Venture Capital Journal (monthly), Capital Publishing Corporation, P.O. Box 348, Wellesley, MA 02181

The Wall Street Journal (daily), 22 Cortlandt Street, New York, NY 10007

Wall Street Transcripts (weekly), 120 Wall Street, New York, NY 10005

The following weekly newsletters are published by *Institutional Investor*, 488 Madison Avenue, New York, NY 10022: *Bank Letter*, *Bond Week*, *Corporate Financing Week*, *Money Management Letter*, *Portfolio Letter*, *Wall Street Letter*.

Professional Associations

Association of M.B.A. Executives
305 Madison Avenue
New York, NY 10017

Securities Industries Association
120 Broadway
New York, NY 10005

INTERVIEWS

Jack Kiernan, Age 27
Associate
Merrill Lynch Capital Markets Investment Banking Division
New York, NY

This job never gets boring, and if it ever does, I'll look for another career. It may get a little intense at times, but I find it a lot of fun and a wonderful challenge. I am dealing with so many intelligent individuals, both within the firm and at client companies, and that's very appealing.

There's a tremendous sense of competition, too. Once upon a time I thought I was going to be a pro golfer; I even played on the U.S. amateur circuit. The willingness to devote time and energy to one thing with the goal of coming out on top, as well as the team and individualistic aspects of competing as a golfer, prepared me well for the investment banking business, strange as that may sound.

I chose investment banking after graduating from Harvard Business School and working one summer as an associate at Merrill

Lynch. Before entering Harvard on a deferred admission from Dartmouth, I worked for two years at Manufacturers Hanover Trust Company in their corporate lending area, doing credit analysis. This work experience was critical for me; not only did the experience of working make me get much more out of business school, but it helped me personally to look at a more aggressive career area. My summer exposure to investment banking really turned me on, and I knew I had found a good place to use all my capabilities.

What I love is that, as an investment banker, I can go in and say to a client, "Look what I can do for you," and, in fact, from day one as an entry-level associate, you're pretty much directly involved with the client and part of a team of two or three others who are each more experienced and have more responsibility in the firm. There is still a lot of "grunt" work, of course, but you get increasingly more responsibility as quickly as you demonstrate that you can handle it.

I work fairly long hours, longer than most people probably. It's not the amount of time that makes it tricky really; it's the way that it changes all the time. I could work two days in a row until midnight, and then work fairly regular hours the next two days. Then you have to add in the travel, and each week differs on that, too.

My typical day begins at about 8 A.M. when I arrive at the office and try to take a quick look at the day's *Wall Street Journal* and the *New York Times*. I usually have two or three projects that are in various stages to handle on any given day, which keeps things interesting. I may have numbers to analyze, reports to read, meetings with senior personnel and people in different parts of the firm. When things calm down around six, I take stock of things and may work for another hour or two at the office and maybe take some paperwork or reading home with me. Then I could have a client dinner some nights.

I think it's essential to be at ease around people. Also, you can't buckle under pressure. The environment calls for an intelligent, well-balanced approach combined with a high motivation level and an ability to remain unruffled even when things get crazy. And to be successful, you have to enjoy what you're doing. Just making a lot of money, which you certainly can in this business, is not enough for me.

Amy Schiffman, Age 29
Vice President
Shearson Lehman/American Express
New York, NY

As far as I am concerned, the thrill and challenge of investment banking is without equal. I am now in my seventh year with the firm. Although my recent promotion has meant that I am now more concerned with the details of daily operations than with transactions, I still feel the excitement of raising capital for some of the world's largest corporations.

In 1975, I entered Harvard Business School directly from Yale College, where I had majored in economics. During the summer between my two years at business school, I was an associate at what was then called Kuhn, Loeb. I loved the job and (although I did look at other employers) I rejoined the firm in 1977 as a generalist in the corporate finance department. Kuhn, Loeb merged with Lehman Brothers a few months later, and subsequently with Shearson/American Express, becoming the firm that it is today.

Like all new associates, I was exposed to many different types of transactions, worked on a number of accounts, and developed client relationships within specific projects. I worked with clients in several different industries, which gave me a well-rounded background. I also worked heavily with retailers, building an expertise that later proved to be valuable.

As I advanced—I became a vice president after three years—I moved from executing analyses to designing and executing, and then to supervising a team of junior people. I also began to work specifically in the development of new business for the retailing group. My experience with retailers enabled me to identify the best prospective clients. My responsibility was to call selected retailers, introduce myself and the firm, explain our capabilities, and suggest a meeting. I enjoyed a good measure of success.

More than a year ago, I was asked to move into the management side of the firm; as a result, direct client contact has taken less of my time. Together with a managing director and a senior managing director, I am administrating the corporate finance department. This department has over three hundred professionals who provide general client services to a range of industries.

I am chiefly responsible for assigning work, establishing client teams, and providing all the coverage needed for each project. I perform staff appraisals and make salary recommendations and career path determinations. In short, I ensure that my staff produces! I also play a major role in recruitment, which involves travel.

Fortunately, I am not totally removed from client work. I love the challenges of solving problems that have no apparent solutions and of having to think on my feet. When you are dealing with millions of dollars, every decision must be correct. A responsible person feels this pressure to perform twenty-four hours a day—it is like being in a pressure cooker—and it makes investment banking one of the most rigorous, but satisfying, careers imaginable.

MANAGEMENT CONSULTING

IN today's highly competitive, fast-changing market, companies are looking to outside experts to help them improve their productivity and profit margins. A growing number of management consulting firms provide those experts. Established firms are adding personnel, opening new branches, and developing new areas of expertise. If you have a strong sense of organization and the knack for seeing through problems and devising innovative solutions, you may well want to investigate this profession.

The field is highly competitive, both for beginners and for experienced professionals. Consultants must demonstrate their effectiveness on each and every job; and client companies have become highly selective about whom they retain for their projects. Consultants are under constant pressure to do top quality work and, later on, to bring new business to the firm. Those who survive the competition to get jobs can expect long hours and extensive travel, balanced by excellent salaries, high status, and continuing professional challenge.

Success in management consulting depends on your ability to bring together a complex combination of skills and attitudes. Besides a personality that thrives on competition, you need to be a creative problem-solver, adept at interaction with people, stimulated by constant change and new challenges, flexible about hours and travel, and able to cope with budgets and deadlines.

Consulting is a high-energy career. Even though you may develop an area of expertise, each consulting project is unique. Your analytic, communication, and people- and project-management skills are constantly tested and stretched. It can take from six to ten years just to establish your maximum capability.

Aside from doing a top job for clients, a seasoned professional consultant must be able to take criticism and make good use of it; consultants are often on the receiving end. Also, you must have the confidence and assertiveness to sell your ability, win clients' trust, and attract new business. Successful consulting calls for intuition, diplomacy, and plenty of reading between the lines. The recommendations you make can mean cuts in personnel or pay, or even a major company restructuring. In essence, you are being paid to be critical of the company, yet you must also make your recommendations palatable to the managers you deal with.

Management consulting is a service offered to companies and organizations in both the private and the public sector. There are about 3500 management consulting firms in the United States and Canada today, plus several thousand independent consultants. The consultant, often assisted by a project team, works with inside managers to define and analyze a problem; then researches and recommends solutions, and sometimes helps to implement the change. The ultimate goal of the consulting process is to improve the client's operational, economic, and managerial performance.

Management consultants deal with clients in all industries, in the public as well as the private sector, examining any and all functional areas. For the most part, the qualifications, career paths, and workstyles of entry-level consultants are similar; however, the work you do varies greatly depending on the area of business on which you focus. The major areas of specialization for management consultants are compensation, financial planning and control, general management, information management, management of human resources, manufacturing, marketing, physical distribution, research and development, and strategic planning.

Increasingly, consultants specialize not only in these major areas but in new subspecialties. Some consultants remain generalists, although this is not the norm. In any case, the basic skills and abilities needed by consultants remain the same.

The application of computer technology to business has generated a whole new area of career opportunities for management consultants. Today only computers can store, retrieve, and process the huge amounts of information that large companies generate, and computer software represents an entirely new order of management tools. The electronic advances of the eighties demand new kinds of business expertise; they continue to create opportunities for consultants to help companies design management information systems and manage their information processing.

Approximately 12 percent of all new M.B.A.s go directly into consulting work; others follow after acquiring corporate or industry experience. Most firms prefer applicants with prior work experience and specific industry expertise. Your career path may require time in the corporate world, either before or after business school, in order for you to be considered qualified by a consulting firm. However, there are opportunities for generalists with strong analytic and communications skills. In either case, it's critical to convince potential employers and clients that you have more than theories to offer, that you can come up with concrete, realistic solutions to real-world business problems.

A final word about what to expect in this field. Clients are willing to pay high fees to get the best possible brains, skills, and advice. In turn, salaries at consulting firms are high in order to attract the best and the brightest, and also to compensate for the heavy intrusions the job makes into your personal life. Dedication to each job at hand is essential, and client feedback about your performance will most certainly affect your progress in your own firm.

Job Outlook

Job Openings Will Grow: Faster than average

Competition for Jobs: Keen

New Job Opportunities: One of the fastest-growing specialties in the consulting industry is management of information systems. Managers want advice on what equipment to invest in, which of the computerized management systems will enhance their operations, and how to train their staffs. Consulting expertise is also increasingly in demand in the following areas, which are expanding or growing in complexity: energy, employee compensation, hospital administration and health care, transportation (especially the recently deregulated airlines industry), financial management, and strategic planning.

Geographic Job Index

About 40 percent of all firms are located in the major cities stretching between Washington, DC, and Boston, MA. The large firms often have branch offices in other cities in the United States and some have branches abroad as well. New branch offices continue to open up wherever business growth occurs.

Other large concentrations of firms are found in the Chicago, IL, area, on the West Coast, and in the Southwest, particularly in Dallas, TX, Houston, TX, and Denver, CO. More business is locating in the Atlanta, GA, area, and there is consequently a growing number of consultants there. Many smaller cities have private practitioners or smaller firms specializing in the particular needs of local industry and businesses.

Who the Employers Are

FULL-SERVICE FIRMS handle a variety of clients and offer assistance at various levels of management and in a number of functional areas, including manufacturing, distribution, marketing, finance, personnel, and systems. Full-service firms may be large or small and are in a position to adapt their services as the market changes.

SPECIALIZED MANAGEMENT CONSULTING FIRMS are usually medium-size or smaller and provide expertise in a single industry, functional area or geographic region.

BIG EIGHT ACCOUNTING FIRMS, through their management consulting divisions, are among the approximately 200 companies that do about 80 percent of the business in the field.

Major Employers

FULL-SERVICE FIRMS
American Management Systems, Inc., New York, NY
Theodore Barry & Associates, Los Angeles, CA
Booz, Allen & Hamilton, New York, NY
Cresap, McCormick and Paget, Inc., New York, NY
Harbridge House, New York, NY
A. T. Kearney, Chicago, IL
Arthur D. Little, Inc., Cambridge, MA
McKinsey & Co., New York, NY
Management Analysis Center, Cambridge, MA
The Reliance Consulting Group, Inc., New York, NY
Science Management Corp., Bridgewater, NJ
SRI International, Menlo Park, CA
Temple, Barker & Sloan, Lexington, MA

BIG EIGHT ACCOUNTING FIRMS WITH MANAGEMENT CONSULTING DIVISIONS
Arthur Andersen & Company, Chicago, IL
Coopers & Lybrand, New York, NY
Deloitte, Haskins & Sells, New York, NY
Ernst & Whinney, Cleveland, OH

Peat, Marwick, Mitchell & Company, New York, NY
Price, Waterhouse, New York, NY
Touche Ross & Company, New York, NY
Arthur Young & Company, New York, NY

SPECIALIZED FIRMS

Bain Associates (Strategic Planning), Boston, MA
Boston Consulting Group (Strategic Planning), Boston,
    MA
A.S. Hansen (Compensation), Lake Bluff, IL
The Hay Group (Compensation), Philadelphia, PA
Hewitt Associates (Compensation), Lincolnshire, IL
Index Systems (Information Systems) Cambridge, MA
William M. Mercer, Inc. (Compensation), New York, NY
Strategic Planning Associates (Strategic Planning),
    Washington, DC
Towers, Perrin, Forster & Crosby (Compensation), New
    York, NY

How to Break into the Field

Hiring practices vary a great deal. Most firms consider prior business experience absolutely essential. Some hire a certain percentage of M.B.A.s right out of school; some give preference to interns. Unless you are at the top of your class in a prestigious business school, count on having to acquire work experience in addition to your M.B.A.

It's good strategic planning to find out which firms handle the kinds of clients and projects that especially interest you, and to tailor your courses and work experience to firms in that area. The vast majority of firms expect knowledge and experience in a specific field. Specialized firms look for applicants who have been working for several years in their area or who acquired such experience between college and business school. Even general firms prefer candidates with some hands-on experience. And although the Big Eight accounting firms are known for hiring M.B.A.s right out of school, that doesn't always hold true.

It is very important, therefore, to research potential employers and learn their hiring preferences. Study the consulting firms' brochures collected by your placement office or directly by you. Seek out people who can offer specific inside information: alumni now working at firms, former summer interns, college placement staff, on-campus recruiters and personnel representatives at the firms. Don't hesitate to contact a firm directly with specific questions about the kinds of staffs they are looking for. It may also be helpful to attend meetings of management consulting clubs or local professional groups.

At the same time, develop expertise and pursue job opportunities in a particular area or industry. Your work experience will complement your classroom knowledge and increase your contacts in the field.

Many consulting firms offer summer internships for M.B.A. candidates between their first and second years at graduate school. Those who perform well are often offered full-time jobs after graduation. Interviews, set up through your placement office or a firm's own personnel or recruiting department, are helpful in evaluating how well a specific firm would suit you—and vice versa. Be prepared to cite work experience as well as academic qualifications at these encounters.

International Job Opportunities

Though opportunities exist, they are not plentiful and they often depend on whether a firm has been able to find qualified nationals for their overseas offices. Americans are the second choice, because it is easier to foster trust between client and consultant when the consultant is at home in a country's culture and legal system, and fluent in the language.

However, there are exceptions. Americans may be hired for the firm's foreign branches abroad. A U.S. employee may have special expertise that would justify a brief foreign assignment. Because of an ongoing relationship with a worldwide client, a consultant may be required to travel in the course of a project covering more than one country.

Without exception, these opportunities become available to

those with considerable experience, rather than to entry-level people. However, if international consulting really interests you, find out which firms are more likely to provide such opportunities later on. Note their client lists and the locations of their branch offices. See if they deal with a variety of U.S. multinational firms. Close business ties to governments and the United Nations are also indications of an international perspective. If you are serious about working in a foreign country as a management consultant, it is critical that your knowledge of that country's language be as good as that of a native.

For lists of firms with international concerns, see the *Consultants News Directory* and the company brochures in your placement office file or write the Association of Management Consulting Firms (ACME). (Address listed at the end of this chapter under "Professional Associations.")

THE WORK

Qualifications

Personal: Ability to analyze, diagnose, and synthesize. Facility for defining the essence of a problem quickly. Finding workable solutions. Dealing well with people. Handling a number of projects at the same time. Ability to speak and write persuasively. Diplomacy. Innate sales ability. Proven leadership skills. Zest for competition. Dedication and drive, to put in long hours and develop new business.

Professional: Broad business knowledge. In-depth knowledge and experience in a particular industry or functional area.

Career Paths

LEVEL	JOB TITLE	EXPERIENCE NEEDED
Entry	Consultant or associate	M.B.A. and previous work experience.
2	Project director or engagement manager	1-3 years
3	Principal consultant, senior consultant, or junior partner	4-7 years
4	Senior partner, vice president	8-12 years

Job Responsibilities

Entry Level

THE BASICS: Compiling data for memos, reports, and studies. Research, including personal interviews, document reviews, flow charting, organizational charting, and evaluating previous studies.

MORE CHALLENGING DUTIES: Assisting with analysis, solution and implementation. Some direct client contact and travel.

Moving Up

Once you have advanced to a more senior level and are considered a senior member of the firm, you will head project teams and have continual contact with clients. You are expected to solve problems, develop new client business, write final reports, and make client presentations. Junior or senior partners have significant management and administrative duties, concentrating even more on project development. Partners also manage relationships within the firm as well as with clients, and share in the firm's profits.

ADDITIONAL INFORMATION

Salaries

	LOW	AVERAGE	HIGH
Associate	$13,000	$ 27,000	$ 48,000
Engagement manager	15,000	37,000	77,000
Principal consultant	23,000	50,000	140,000
Junior partner	29,000	71,900	180,000
Senior partner	30,000	104,000	305,000

Working Conditions

Hours: Consultants must be prepared to work long, often irregular hours. Initially many consultants put in 50- to 60-hour weeks. Because entry-level salaries are so high, firms expect employees to work substantial overtime on the assumption that this is the only way projects get done and new consultants learn the business.

Environment: Offices are attractive and comfortable, consistent with any image of competence and success. New consultants may share offices at first, then advance to a small private office. The atmosphere is often highly competitive. "If you don't grow, you go," creates constant pressure for consultants, but those who are happy in the business consider this atmosphere stimulating and challenging.

Workstyle: Initially consultants spend a lot of time researching in the office, advancing to on-location research and interviews, meeting with clients and communicating the results of studies. In the office, there may be many meetings—planning proposals and presentations, and conferring with clients and the other members of a project team.

Travel: As the consultant progresses, travel will become more and more a routine part of the job. Up to 60 percent of the experienced consultant's week can be spent with the client company, whose offices and plants may be anywhere in the country—doing research, meeting with people, and ultimately presenting a final report. Destinations can be regional or nationwide.

Internships

Many informal internship arrangements are worked out between students and employers. Find out which firms do this by talking with your placement office, querying firms yourself, contacting ACME, and talking to senior students. Many firms offer students summer employment between their first and second year at business school. Most recruit on campus, so you can contact your placement office for information. However, contacting firms on your own initiative can bring good results.

Some major firms co-sponsor deferred admissions programs with business schools; an employee works in the firm, then goes to business school full-time and returns to the firm after earning an M.B.A. These students are excellent sources of information about opportunities at the firms where they've worked.

Recommended Reading

BOOKS

Bradford's Directory of Marketing Research and Management Consultants in the United States and the World, Bradfords, VA: 1984

The Complete Consultant: A Roadmap to Success by Hubert Bermont, Bermont Books: 1982

Consultants and Consulting Organizations Directory, Gale Research Company: 1984

Consulting Handbook by Howard L. Shenson, H. L. Shenson, Inc.: 1982

PERIODICALS
Management Science (monthly), Institute of Management Sciences, 146 Westminster Street, Providence, RI 02903

Professional Associations

Association of Internal Management Consultants
P.O. Box 155
Cranford, NJ 07016

Association of Management Consultants
500 North Michigan Avenue
Chicago, IL 60611

Association of Management Consulting Firms (ACME)
230 Park Avenue
Suite 1605
New York, NY 10169

Institute of Management Consultants (IMC)
19 West 44th Street
New York, NY 10036

The Institute of Management Science
290 Westminster Street
Providence, RI 02093

Society of Professional Management Consultants
162 Eagle Street
Englewood, NJ 07631

INTERVIEWS

Lin Kroeger
Vice President
Link Associates, Secaucus, NY

When I was 12, I decided to go into the theater, and nothing was going to stop me. Management consulting might not seem like a logical progression, but I now use many of the skills I learned from studying theater—especially my ability to present myself and to analyze personalities.

Halfway through the College of William and Mary, I switched my major from theater to interdisciplinary studies and became certified to teach English, which I did for three years. I have translated this experience also into my consulting work. Later I taught in the writing program at Cornell's Graduate School of Business and Public Administration. Then, when I applied for nonacademic jobs, I was offered a position at Arthur Andersen, a Big Eight accounting firm. They were developing their professional education division, and I had special skills—writing and the teaching of writing—they were looking for.

At Andersen, I was at their professional education center at St. Charles, IL, and because of the growth of the division I was able to get an intensive education in business and corporate training. I was part of the management development group, working as a course manager and instructor, and I traveled about 80 percent of the time. I also began to do a lot of internal consulting and frequently worked with clients. I was the firm's expert on writing, sometimes specializing in areas such as the documentation of policies and procedures and proposal writing. I traveled a great deal and eventually developed a close working relationship with the woman who co-founded our consulting firm.

After two years, what had been a very open, fluid situation became more structured as the division itself became more structured. I wanted to do more consulting, so I left and worked with a small firm for six months before starting a business with Randy O'Neill. We founded Link Associates to specialize in communications consulting—especially customized communications training. We have one associate, and as of April 1984 a third partner in the firm, and plan to continue expanding as our client base grows. We want to remain a small firm, but not a small operation. Originally, I was responsible for much of the selling and marketing, but now we all share responsibility for developing business, designing and delivering seminars, and consulting. We bring in other consultants when we need other specialists or more people for a project.

Usually, I work anywhere from 50 to 80 hours a week and travel 30 to 80 percent of the month. It is not unusual for me to be up at 5 A.M. for a two-hour drive to a meeting with a client. And every week is different. Much of the time I'm catching planes or driving from one city to another, meeting with clients, conducting seminars, and giving presentations. A slow week means I'm in the office for two or three days to arrange sales and follow-up meetings, develop ideas for presentations and seminars, prepare material for a seminar, check with clients by phone, catch up with correspondence, meet with our accountants, and so on. Slow weeks are just as long as other ones, but they go at a slightly slower pace.

One weekend, I spent all day Saturday at a printer's preparing for seminars that I conducted in New Jersey and Washington, DC, on Sunday and Monday—so that I could return to New York to give a presentation on Tuesday.

Sure, there are weeks when the time, energy, and travel commitment far exceed the rewards professionally and monetarily, but there are also times when people share things with us and discover abilities they hadn't been using before. It's a special feeling when someone tells you, "Now I understand what to do," and then does it right in front of you. Encouraging that growth process is a lot of what our firm is about.

It may be that because of my unusual background educationally and professionally, I'm able to bring together a lot of different skills I began to acquire when I was 12. Yes, I thought I'd be using them in a different profession, but I enjoy having control over whether I work, and I believe I am using most of them to be an effective consultant.

Charles Lee, Age 40
Principal Consultant
Towers, Perrin, Forster & Crosby, Cleveland, OH

My intention was to go into the human side of business, and working as a management consultant has fulfilled that goal. Essentially I'm a problem-solver, and I use all the interactive skills available—listening, communicating information, and working with a client toward a common goal.

My prior work experience prepared me well. After college I served in the Peace Corps and worked for several government agencies. Then I earned my M.B.A. at the Wharton School of Business, worked for Exxon as a personnel analyst, and became a personnel manager. My training and experience in that field made me attractive to Towers, Perrin, Forster & Crosby, a large New York-based firm that I joined seven years ago.

My first assignments as an associate were designed to use my knowledge of the personnel area and, equally as important, to teach me how the firm worked, its style and methods of operation. I didn't travel much at first or meet many clients face-to-face. It was a "molding" period, during which you and your supervisors assess your strengths, build on them, and see more clearly where you fit in the firm.

Even though I had prior experience and was not quite the new kid on the block, I still had to learn the tools of the trade as well as the standards of quality of my company. Usually it takes a few years before management is ready to offer you to a client as an expert. Clients are paying for expertise, and so your fees have to pay your dues.

When clients retain me, they retain me personally, as well as the firm. I write my own reports and proposals. I confer with people doing similar salalry administration work. I review interview notes, analyze them, and check reference information. Then I offer the clients solutions and my recommendations on how to use them in the best possible way. That's what they want from me.

Many of the analyzing and writing tasks are done on weekends, when I am not developing business on behalf of the firm, which is one of my chief responsibilities as a principal consultant. In a typical week, I am out of my office some portion of every day, traveling to existing clients or prospecting new ones.

There are several ways that I drum up business. A successfully completed assignment often results in a referral, which I follow up. To keep myself visible, I write articles, give speeches, and attend workshops. I also contact prospective clients and feel them out. There is always a stage of exploration before an assignment is approved and I nearly always have to submit a written proposal. I may get an assignment immediately, or it may take a year to come through. I think of myself as perpetually curious. I want to find solutions to problems, and each one is a new challenge for me. I have to be able to show clients I understand their problems and can devise appropriate solutons.

I enjoy the collegiality of problem-solving. It's very exciting to help people work more effectively. And it enables me to grow, too; as people's needs change so do solutions to human resources problems. I use both humanistic and financial skills to help companies use people and resources efficiently.

I'm grateful for the experience I've had. Some firms hire you more for your brains or school standing, and you either make it or you're out. Others, like TPF & C, select more carefully and help you make it. That has made all the difference in my career—we offered each other something and we have both benefited.

MANUFACTURING

M ANUFACTURING is the leading industry in the United States. It encompasses a wide range of industrial classifications, each of which produces goods by hand or machine for the consumer or industrial market. The United States rose to world leadership in manufacturing during World War I and has maintained that position ever since.

According to the U.S. Census Bureau, the leading manufactured products in the United States are chemicals, electric and electronic equipment, fabricated metal products, primary metals, printed materials, rubber and plastic products, and transportation equipment.

Approximately 24 percent of the nation's income is derived from manufacturing—and this area employs about 22 percent of the country's labor force. Manufacturing offers outstanding opportunities to M.B.A.s. The Association of M.B.A. Executives, Inc., reports that 40 percent of the M.B.A. graduates in 1981-82 obtained jobs in manufacturing.

Although the Northeast and Midwest have traditionally been the strongest regions for manufacturing in the United States, the fastest growing areas since the mid-1950s have been the Southwest, the South, and California. The Northeast is known for its concentration of clothing, electronics equipment, food processing, and printing plants; the Midwest for its automotive, heavy industry, iron and steel plants; the Gulf States for petrochemicals; California for high-technology industries, aerospace, and food products; Dallas-Fort Worth, TX, Wichita, KS, and Atlanta, GA, for the aircraft industry.

New developments in technology have had considerable impact on the manufacturing industry. Such advances as automated material handling, robots, and computerized production techniques have made equipment and many long-used manufacturing techniques obsolete. Management and labor have required retraining, and plants have required modernization. Companies that have been unwilling or unable to adapt to the technological changes have found themselves competing unfavorably, both with other American companies and with companies abroad. Rising costs have led a number of companies to relocate their facilities to more rural settings where labor is cheaper and the tax structure more favorable. Furthermore, concern for environmental pollution and energy waste have required management to set up special departments or to hire consultants so that they can make appropriate changes to conform to the law and cut down on energy waste.

New M.B.A.s—bright, energetic, well-motivated, and trained in modern management practice—have a contribution to make to the industry. Most of the jobs available to M.B.A.s with nontechnical backgrounds fall into two career areas:

- **Marketing and Market Research**
- **Finance**

Marketing and market research involves maximizing the way in which the company's product is presented in the marketplace; and finance involves managing the company's money and assets for profit and growth. These job functions are discussed in detail later in the chapter. However, two additional functions are note-worthy: industrial relations/human resources management, and procurement and supply. These jobs are in much shorter supply than marketing and finance positions, but some manufacturing companies do look for qualified M.B.A. candidates. For jobs in procurement and supply, a technical background can be an advantage.

Because the manufacturing industry is so broad, the discussion in this chapter is limited to five key areas: automobiles, chemicals, food processing, pharmaceuticals, and household products.

Job Outlook

Job Openings will Grow: Little change

Competition for Jobs: Keen
Many of the top manufacturing companies are extremely selective in choosing new M.B.A.s for employment. Chrysler Corporation reports: "We probably look at eight to ten candidates to get one good one. It's basically a buyer's market." Some companies concentrate their recruiting efforts exclusively at top-tier business schools and note that unsolicited résumés have a very small chance for success. Other companies, however, send their interviewers to 10 or 20 schools across the country and are more interested in locating good candidates, whatever the source. Well-qualified individuals with a strong academic record and related industrial experience will be at an advantage in the search for entry-level jobs.

New Job Opportunities: The recent recession forced many companies in the manufacturing industry to make drastic employment cuts. In the automotive industry, for example, although job levels are still moderated by the tendency to remain "lean and mean" in staff levels, there is an ongoing need to build solid management. Manufacturing plants are undergoing modernization programs to reduce production costs, turn out smaller, more fuel-efficient vehicles, and become more competitive in the marketplace.

In the chemical industry, cost reduction programs have resulted in plant closings and reductions in inventory and personnel. However, the general outlook for the industry is optimistic, except for companies in the agricultural area, which have been adversely affected by a strong U.S. dollar, low exports, and government farm programs resulting in reductions in planted acreage and reduced consumption of pesticides and fertilizer. However, research and development spending in the industry, although still not at 1981 or 1982 levels, is expected to increase.

The food processing industry will continue to enjoy a relatively healthy economic outlook, continuing its high operating earnings history of the past ten years. However, profits are expected to grow more slowly as government farm programs have an impact on grain prices and consumers continue to resist price increases at the supermarket and to purchase lower-priced goods. Also, government and consumer group pressure has led to new regulations on ingredient safety, labeling requirements, and container legislation, putting new demands on the industry.

The pharmaceutical industry has enjoyed healthy growth for the past ten years as a result of increasing numbers of older citizens and their expanding health needs; increased government funding for health care; and the introduction of new drug products and health care items. Problems facing the industry focus on the area of drug approvals: the Food and Drug Administration is being pressured by drug producers to speed up the drug approval process, while consumer pressure groups are agitating to tighten requirements and procedures in the aftermath of several fatalities involving FDA-approved drugs. The industry's emphasis on research and development has resulted in the successful introduction of a record number of new products into the marketplace. Demand for health care equipment is expected to continue, with a strong market in the area of electromedical equipment.

The anticipated growth areas for the household products industry during the next few years include generic brands, heavy-duty liquid laundry detergents, liquid soap, and specialty soaps. In cosmetics and toiletries, natural cosmetics, men's fragrances, and ethnic cosmetics are expected to be strong markets. This industry is especially responsive to advertising, marketing, new product development, and improvement programs as companies vie for a larger share of the market. Government regulations are having an impact on product acceptance as ingredients in soaps, detergents, and cosmetics are subjected to scrutiny for their environmental and consumer safety.

If the manufacturing area that interests you is not covered in this chapter, you may wish to familiarize yourself with it through a number of books, available in your local or college library, that offer excellent listings of professional associations and trade publications. These include *The Ayer Directory of Publications; Business Publications Rates and Data; Encyclopedia of Associations; Magazine Industry Market Place; National Trade & Professional Associations of the United States; Ulrich's International Periodicals Directory*; and *Where to Find Business Information*. Full details can be found under "Recommended Reading" at the end of this chapter.

Geographic Job Index

The leading manufacturing states according to the U.S. Census Bureau are California, Illinois, Indiana, Michigan, New Jersey, New York, Ohio, Pennsylvania, and Texas.

Who the Employers Are

AUTOMOBILES are a major manufactured item. This industry produces motor vehicles (buses, passenger cars, and trucks) and auto parts, both original and replacement.

CHEMICALS produced by companies in this industry are basic chemicals (including chlor-alkalis, industrial gases, inorganic and organic chemicals); synthetic materials (including synthetic fibers, plastics, and synthetic rubber); and specific chemical products (such as cosmetics, detergents, drugs, explosives, fertilizers, paints, pesticides, and soaps).

FOOD PROCESSING represents more than 13 percent of the nations's manufacturing output. This industry includes six basic product areas: alcoholic beverages, bakery products, bottled and canned soft drinks, canned and frozen fruits and vegetables, dairy processing, and meat and meat packaging.

PHARMACEUTICALS has been one of the five most profitable industries in the United States for more than 20 years. It includes companies that specialize in prescription (ethical) drugs, over-the-counter (proprietary) drugs, and health care equipment.

HOUSEHOLD PRODUCTS include a wide range of manufactured products from soaps and detergents (the largest group) to bleaches, cleaning compounds, floor waxes, and toiletries.

Major Employers

AUTOMOBILES
>   Chrysler Corporation, Detroit, MI
>   Ford Motor Company, Dearborn, MI
>   General Motors Corporation, Detroit, MI

CHEMICALS
>   American Cyanamid Company, Wayne, NJ
>   E.I. DuPont DeNemours & Co., Inc., Wilmington, DE
>   W.R. Grace & Company, New York, NY

FOOD PROCESSING
>   General Foods Corporation, White Plains, NY
>   General Mills, Inc., Minneapolis, MN
>   The Nestlé Company, Inc., White Plains, NY

PHARMACEUTICALS
>   Abbot Laboratories, North Chicago, IL
>   Baster Travenol Laboratories, Inc., Deerfield, IL
>   Eli Lilly & Company, Indianapolis, IN

HOUSEHOLD PRODUCTS
>   The Clorox Company Inc., Oakland, CA
>   Johnson & Johnson, New Brunswick, NJ
>   Schering Plough Corporation, Kenilworth, NJ

For additional information on manufacturing companies, several references are particularly helpful. The *Thomas Register of American Manufacturers* offers an extensive multivolume listing of American manufacturers. *The Career Opportunity Index* organizes companies by location in a series of regional editions. *The M.B.A. Employment Guide* provides a summary of each of the hundred leading M.B.A. employers, including company background, products, current recruitment opportunities, and financial information. An alphabetical employer index, cross-referenced by primary business function and location, highlights approximately 1500 American companies. If you are currently enrolled in an M.B.A. program, check your graduate school library and placement office for reference material. If you are a college student, you may find helpful resources on campus, especially in the business school or department.

How to Break into the Field

A substantial number of entry-level M.B.A.s get their first job through business school placement office referrals and interviews on campus. Major manufacturing corporations are looking for competent people to be managers. If they are impressed with your capability, they will often create a job for you rather than miss the opportunity to employ you. Candidates with previous work experience in the industry and an understanding of its problems have a definite advantage. If you are a first-year business school student and have a preference for a specific industry, contact the company's director of college recruitment or personnel director to inquire about summer employment. Many manufacturing companies offer summer internships to M.B.A. students. This is an excellent opportunity for you to obtain firsthand experience in the industry, get a good idea of what jobs are available, and make valuable contacts for future full-time employment.

College recruiting personnel offer a few tips on interviewing for the M.B.A.: have a clear idea of your business goals and be able to explain your reasons for wanting to work for that specific company; and be prepared to discuss the area for which you are best suited. Candidates who are vague about their business objectives and display ignorance about the industry and the company interviewing them produce a negative reaction.

If you have high career goals for yourself, be sure to determine the company's basic management orientation when you are looking for your entry-level job. In some companies, the career path to the top is through marketing; in others, finance is the route to follow. If you have executive management aspirations, you may wish to look for a company that emphasizes your specialty in its management structure.

International Job Opportunities

Opportunities for international assignments are rare for entry-level American-born M.B.A.s. If you are interested in working overseas, you should seek employment in a company with international divisions. It usually takes three to five years or more of successful job experience before a corporation considers moving an executive to a foreign division.

However, foreign nationals who obtain an M.B.A. from an American graduate school are in demand at corporations with international operations. For example, Johnson & Johnson's International M.B.A. Development Program specifically looks for outstanding foreign-national M.B.A. graduates. The foreign graduates are trained at corporate headquarters for placement in management positions in 150 worldwide companies. Eli Lilly & Company looks to recruit foreign nationals for its overseas assignments as well.

MARKETING AND MARKET RESEARCH

Marketing and market research provide a critical link to the sales, production, and finance departments of your company. In large corporations, the two job functions are distinct career areas. Market research provides technical expertise in data collection and analysis and is technical in nature; marketing makes decisions based on market research data and is managerial in orientation. In smaller companies, the two areas may be combined.

As a marketing staff person you will help evaluate every product or service of your company and provide data and recommendations that will maximize the product's acceptance by the consumer. You will help determine whether a new product should be introduced, who is likely to buy it, and what price should be charged. Marketing departments cope with such problems as what features the product should have and how it should be packaged. You will be heavily involved with advertising and public relations, making decisions on how the product should be introduced, what media should be used, and what image of the company should be portrayed. In the case of existing products, you will examine customer attitudes: whether users like the product's design and performance, whether they are having any problems, and what improvements, if any, are needed. Are there additional applications of the product that could be implemented, or new markets to approach? How does the company's market share compare with that of its competitors?

Advances in technology have brought vast quantities of data within easy reach. Modern communications links have shortened the distance from customers to suppliers. Your use of the computer will make it possible to hypothesize, analyze, and apply the results of market studies of product, audience, and price, and ensure that your company is competitive in the marketplace.

Qualifications

Personal: Excellent interpersonal skills. Highly motivated. Broad-based background.

Professional: Excellent organizational skills. Good oral and written communications skills. In-depth understanding of business management. Knowledge of statistics. Consumer empathy.

Career Paths

LEVEL	JOB TITLE	EXPERIENCE NEEDED
Entry	Assistant marketing/ product manager	M.B.A.
2	Associate product manager	1-2 years
3	Product manager	3-4 years
4	Product group manager	6 years
5	Category manager 8 years	
6	Marketing manager	10-11 years
7	General manager	13-15 years

Job Responsibilities

Entry Level

THE BASICS: Writing memos and reports on product performance, customer reaction, or other variables affecting your product. Meeting with package suppliers and designers. Liaison with public relations or advertising department or agency.

MORE CHALLENGING DUTIES: Working on analyses, budgets, and key strategies. Doing volume planning. Assessing competitive position. Developing promotional materials.

Moving Up

As an associate product manager, you'll be in charge of media plans and overall strategies in the development of advertising. A small brand name product may also be under your supervision.

The next series of advancements will depend not only on your capability to perform well in your job and your readiness to move on, but on openings as well. In a food packaging company, for example, the product manager slot can be the career path to the top positions in the corporation—chairperson or general management executives. As a product manager, your scope of influence will have expanded to put you in charge of setting overall brand strategies and advertising policies for one product or several related brands. The next step up is product group manager, where you will supervise all the activities of the assistant and associate product managers and be responsible for volume, profit, and financial planning for your brands.

Depending on your company's size, management structure, and industry, your next career move might be category manager, marketing manager, and finally general manager. A fast-track person in a major food packaging corporation can move from entry level to division marketing manager in ten years. If you are very competent and the next career slot in marketing is filled, you may be moved into the corporate area for a staff position in marketing.

In larger corporations, the area of market research offers additional career opportunities for the M.B.A. Market research involves analysis of marketing and economic data, and developing and conducting studies regarding purchasing attitudes and the company's advertising image. Entry-level candidates begin as market research analysts, progressing to market research manager, group market research manager and ultimately director of market research. Analysts supervise clerical and data tabulating functions; collaborate with managers on special assignments; and specify studies and provide data for the product business units. Marketing M.B.A.s can move into this area as an alternative career path.

In pharmaceutical or chemical companies, entry-level marketing candidates can look forward to firsthand experience in field sales for three to six months. In some cases, you may serve as sales rep in a territory and spend your first year selling the company's product before returning to the home office for a position as product manager or in market research. If you have an interest in and an aptitude for sales management, you might progress to field sales manager.

FINANCE

Financial personnel are responsible for the economic health of a corporation. They manage the company's money and its tangible and intangible assets, in the context of the capital market, the corporate tax structure, and prevailing economic conditions.

As an associate financial analyst, your analytical ability will help you identify key business problems, evaluate alternatives, and develop logical conclusions and recommendations. You will be involved with budgets, capital expense proposals, financial statements, operating costs, sales forecasts, and long-range plans.

You will find many challenging opportunities within the financial area of the corporation. Using the latest data acquisition techniques and analysis methods, you will interact with research and management areas and work with marketing personnel. You will be involved in many phases of the company's operations, ranging from corporate departments to operating divisions and manufacturing plants. At some firms the new M.B.A. employee is assigned to an experienced staff member who supervises a planned rotation assignment covering such areas as financial analysis, general and cost accounting, marketing accounting, and analysis and financial planning. At other companies you might be assigned to a single area where you are supervised by an experienced analyst.

Qualifications

Personal: Confident. Self-motivated. Flexible. Interacts well with people.

Professional: Well-organized. Excellent decision-making skills. Good oral and written communication. Broad understanding of business management. Accounting and computer skills.

Career Paths

LEVEL	JOB TITLE	EXPERIENCE NEEDED
Entry	Associate financial analyst or finance management trainee	M.B.A.
2	Staff financial analyst	1 year
3	Senior analyst	3-5 years
4	Department head	5-7 years
5	Manager	9-10 years
6	Director	12-15 years

Job Responsibilities

Entry Level

THE BASICS: Learning the financial structure of the corporation. Writing reports.

MORE CHALLENGING DUTIES: Conducting field audits. Developing and administering budgets. Working with marketing personnel as part of a project team. Initiating special studies. Using computer simulation and forecasting techniques.

Moving Up

As you move on to staff financial analyst, you will have additional responsibility in organizing and completing jobs. You will continue to do monthly financial reporting and profit planning, but you may be assigned to a different group. You will also help some of the entry-level analysts, assisting them in accomplishing their tasks, and doing some initial training.

You will gain a firmer command of the company's financial structure and operations as you move on to senior analyst. A number of career paths are available at this point. Advancement can be vertical or horizontal—from one financial area to another, or between corporate and divisional units. Depending on your industry, your job might include developing budgets for a manufacturing facility or analyzing the profit potential of future product lines. You might have responsibility for preparing financial data for reports to stockholders. At the department head or manager level you might have the opportunity to move into a smaller affiliate, or be assigned overseas. With each succeeding move you will have a wider span of responsibilities and more people to supervise. If experience with a specific division would be useful at this point in your career, you might be moved from department head to another area of the company and again have the title of senior analyst.

Challenging opportunities are available for advancing M.B.A.s in the tax departments, treasurer's department, and controller areas of the corporation. If your company has an international division, you could move into international operations, working with financing arrangements, planning currency fluctuations, and planning intercompany transactions.

Many companies encourage employee advancement through a program of workshops and seminars designed to hone financial and management skills. Tuition reimbursement plans are also common for approved courses of study at schools and colleges.

ADDITIONAL INFORMATION

Salaries

Entry-level salaries vary widely in manufacturing and can be anywhere from $19,000 to $35,000 per year depending on the company, the industry, the business school you attended, your previous industrial background if any, and location. Salary increases depend on performance, but top-level managers in some industries can earn well into six figures.

Working Conditions

Hours: Manufacturing corporations vary in their working hours for management personnel. Many companies formally start work at 7:30 a.m., especially if manufacturing operations are in progress at the same location. Or they may schedule the work day to begin at 8:30 or 9:30 a.m. In still other businesses, executives may work flex-time hours, setting their own eight-hour work day period, with the approval of their supervisors. It is not uncommon for staff to take work home in the evenings or on the weekends, or to work late during rush periods.

Environment: Depending on the size, location, age, and style of your company, and on whether you are working at corporate headquarters, a field sales office, or in a manufacturing plant, your working facilities and equipment will range from plush to traditional to adequate. You may work in a partitioned area that is part of a large, open work center. Or you might have your own office with desk, chair, and door. In a factory, the working arrangements could be as informal as a desk tucked into a quiet corner at the end of a hall.

Workstyle: As an entry-level marketing analyst, you can expect to spend a reasonable amount of time at your desk, evaluating reports, generating memos, and talking on the phone. You will need to attend meetings and follow up on details to get the job done.

As a financial analyst, you will spend a lot of time at your desk. Data acquisition may require meetings, phone calls, or access to the computer terminal.

Travel: Local travel will be a part of your marketing job, with occasional visits to the ad agency, the printer, or a new product launching site. During your first financial assignment travel will probably be minimal.

Internships

Many manufacturing corporations offer paid summer internships to M.B.A. students. Their recruiting staffs visit business schools to interview graduate students who are seeking employment for the summer following their first year of school.

If you have a special interest, expertise, or experience related to a particular company or field of manufacturing, you may write to the director of personnel or the college recruiting department at the company of your choice. It is a good idea to familiarize yourself with the industry and the company and to include your specific reasons for seeking employment with that company. A successful summer internship provides valuable industrial experience to the M.B.A. and will be an asset when you are ready to apply for full-time employment. In addition, your summer job may lead to an employment offer from that company when you graduate.

Recommended Reading

BOOKS

The Ayer Directory of Publications, IMS Press: Revised annually

Business Publications Rates and Data, Standard Rate and Data: Revised annually

The Career Opportunity Index, Career Research Systems: Revised semi-annually

Encyclopedia of Associations, Gale Research Company: Revised annually

Magazine Industry Marketplace, R.R. Bowker: Revised annually

M.B.A. Employment Guide, Association of M.B.A. Executives: 1984

National Trade and Professional Associations of the United States, Columbia Books: Revised annually

Standard and Poor's Register of Corporations, Directors and Executives, Standard and Poor: Revised annually

Thomas Register of American Manufacturers, Thomas Publishing Company: Revised annually

Ulrich's International Periodicals Directory, R.R. Bowker: Revised annually

Where to Find Business Information by David M. Brownstone and Gordon Carruth, John Wiley and Sons: 1982

PERIODICALS

Dun's Business Month (monthly), 875 Third Avenue, New York, NY 10022

Marketing Communications (monthly), United Business Publications, 475 Park Avenue South, New York, NY 10016

Marketing News (biweekly), American Marketing Association, 222 South Riverside Plaza, Chicago, IL 60606

Marketing Times (bimonthly), Sales and Marketing Executives International, 330 West 42nd Street, New York, NY 10036

Professional Associations

American Finance Association
Graduate School of Business Administration
New York University
100 Trinity Place
New York, NY 10006

American Financial Services Association
1101 Fourteenth Street N.W.
Washington, DC 20005

American Management Association
135 West 50th Street
New York, NY 10020

American Marketing Association
Suite 200, 250 South Wacker Drive
Chicago, IL 60606

American Society for Personnel Administration
30 Park Drive
Berea, OH 44017

Association of M.B.A. Executives, Inc.
305 Madison Avenue
New York, NY 10165

Financial Management Association
University of South Florida
Tampa, FL 33620

Institute of Financial Education
111 East Wacker Drive
Chicago, IL 60601

National Association of Manufacturers
1776 F Street, N.W.
Washington, DC 20006

National Association of Purchasing Management
496 Kinderkamack Road
P.O. Box 418
Oradell, NJ 07649

INTERVIEWS

Lisa Heid, Age 28
Staff Financial Analyst
Eli Lilly & Company, Indianapolis, IN

I had been teaching for three years when I decided to make a job change. After taking a few courses to see if I'd like business, I enrolled as a finance major in a full-time M.B.A. program at Indiana University.

I've been with Eli Lilly for two years. My first job was associate financial analyst for the pharmaceutical division. I was one of two analysts doing forecasting and business planning. The job included reporting actual monthly sales, expenses, and income results to management, and forecasting for the rest of the year. It involved working with numbers and being able to explain and look at issues. Computer skills were essential in managing the amount of data required in this type of management reporting, so I was enrolled in computer orientation classes. These classes, along with some basic systems knowledge from graduate school, allowed me to work with the data base and make minor modifications to existing programs. Other responsibilities included budget analysis for the field and home office departments and solving departmental budget problems as they came up.

After one year I was promoted to staff financial analyst. I remained in the same area and assumed additional responsibility for coordinating, organizing, and completing projects. Six months later I moved to a position in pharmaceutical credit. Although my previous job was entirely home office based, now I traveled about 10 percent of the time, making wholesale visits, performing financial analyses to determine the appropriate credit levels, and writing reports. This job provided an entirely new focus—working with people outside the company, primarily wholesalers and bankers.

I'm now working in the corporate financial group as a staff financial analyst. My responsibilities include budget analysis for the industrial relations and corporate affairs groups. We still get involved with monthly financial reporting and do business planning. A typical day includes a fair amount of phone calls. A part of my job is to gather the necessary information to answer questions posed by the areas I serve as budget analyst. Overall, I perform a financial consultant role for these two corporate groups. About 15 percent of my time is spent in meetings, and I've done some presentations.

Working at Lilly has been a good experience for me. One of the reasons I left the education field was the lack of flexibility. Here I've been able to make changes and take on new challenges. Basically I work from 7:30 a.m. to 5 or 5:30 p.m. There are crunch periods a few times each month when we work longer hours, but I can schedule my vacations and have time for my own leisure activities. The job doesn't create any undue stress. The important thing is to anticipate some of the things management is going to want. At times it is hectic, but I try to be fairly even in my workstyle. I know I push myself when there's a deadline. At those times I seem to have a higher energy level.

I think the key to job success is feeling that the company you choose is where you want to be. Having a good match is important. A lot depends on the working climate and the people you're working with. If you feel that you're not making a contribution, it can be frustrating. It's important to view your work as meaningful and to see it being utilized by management in the decision-making process.

Archbold van Beuren, Age 26
Assistant Marketing Manager
Campbell Soup Company, Camden, NJ

When I graduated with my M.B.A. from Columbia University, I was looking for a job that would offer me room for growth, where I could be part of an organization that has clout and power to change things in the market place and bring benefits to the consumer. I was interviewed by a broad range of companies and picked Campbell Soup because it's a large consumer food company with some of the country's leading brands, and it markets its products around the world.

As an assistant marketing manager, I report to the marketing manager in charge of new product development in the beverage area. My job is to work on new products and help bring them to market. I was put in charge of running two test markets for fruit juice-based beverages. I help decide what we want to test and then oversee the implementation: how much product is needed to conduct the test, shelf placement of product, and consumer promotion events. I also visit the markets. I'm responsible for monitoring 20 supermarkets in two cities. I spend a lot of time handling details for our advertising and promotion campaigns. I review mechanicals at the printer to check that they're right. I work with the ad agency to insure that our products are properly represented in photographs. I may make a content decision at a shoot to make sure that the tone of the commercial reflects the proper image of the company and the brand. Overseeing the budget is also my responsibility. I get a list of our actual expenditures and compare this with our estimates. I project costs for the rest of the year on a month-by-month basis, and if we're going to be over budget, I discuss it with my boss and decide how to get back on budget. I also spend a lot of time setting up research focus groups, writing memos, and coordinating other office activities.

One of the great things about my job is that it's so diverse. There's a new challenge every day. You're always meeting and working with people. Campbell doesn't have a formal training program. It's more like a "deep water policy"; they throw you in and see if you can swim! Like any good job, it's fairly high-pressured. There are good days and bad days when you feel the frustration of having so much to do. You're working with products that are staples for the American consumer, so the company's commitment to quality is very important.

I usually start work at seven-thirty in the morning—the company hours are eight to four-thirty—and leave between six-thirty and seven-thirty at night. Most days are so busy that the only time you can work without interruptions is before and after normal working hours. Occasionally I take work home in the evenings, and one or two weekends a month I spend a few hours at home writing memos or getting through my mail. You do what you have to do to get the job done.

I think my job is fascinating. The most frustrating part is a lack of knowledge at times. There are so many things I want to know but I can't possibly understand right away. But I wouldn't want a job where I didn't learn something every day. As you move up, this increased knowledge allows you to make decisions with greater impact.

SECURITIES

FORTY million people and institutions in the United States alone trade in stocks and bonds. A report on the day's trading, the Dow-Jones Index, is a staple of the evening news broadcast. The business of selling securities is a large and lucrative one; top brokers and analysts earn as much as $400,000 a year. It's easy to see, then, why so many success-oriented people set their sights on Wall Street—a term that long ago came to mean the securities industry as a whole.

The term, of course, derives from the handsome old beaux arts-style building at 11 Wall Street that is the home of the New York Stock Exchange and is linked by half a million miles of telephone and telegraph wires to brokerage offices around the world. This vast communications network enables a buyer in London, England, for example, to purchase stock from a seller in California in a matter of minutes.

There are 6935 brokerage firms in the United States registered with the Securities and Exchange Commission (SEC). Ranging in size from small, two-room operations to multinational giants like Merrill Lynch, they can be found in cities across the country and around the world. New York, NY, however, is the undisputed capital of the securities industry, offering more job opportunities than anyplace else.

But although the New York Stock Exchange, or the Big Board, is by far the largest central marketplace in the United States for securities trading, it's not the only one. The American Exchange is located nearby, and there are several regional exchanges: the Pacific, in San Francisco, CA, the Midwest, in Chicago, IL, and others in Boston, MA, Cincinnati, OH, and Philadelphia, PA.

Not every stock can qualify to be listed on one or more of the country's exchanges (requirements for the New York Stock Exchange are the most rigorous). Stocks are traded by brokers who are members of the exchange on which the stock is listed. (A brokerage house may be—and often is—a member of more than one exchange.)

When a broker receives a call from a client who wishes to buy a particular stock, the purchase order is directed to the floor of the appropriate exchange via computer. The brokerage firm has a representative there, called a floor broker. Every listed stock has a trading post, which is a specific location on the exchange's floor, and the floor broker goes there to ask for a quote—both the highest open bid made for the stock and the lowest available offer. Based on the quote, the broker offers a price, shouting out his or her bid for the number of shares the client wants. A floor broker with shares of that stock to sell calls out a offer to sell at the offered price, and a trade is made. The transaction is recorded immediately and the price of the stock is sent back to the broker's office by computer; the broker in turn relays the information to the client. The order is also sent over the wires and appears on the ticker tape in the office of every firm with a seat on that exchange.

Unlisted stocks are traded over the counter. On an electronic visual display unit the broker can call up information listing the securities firms that trade in the various unlisted stocks, and the trade is then conducted directly by telephone.

Securities firms are currently locked in fierce competition with banks for customers' dollars. Recent federal deregulation permits both of these industries to offer products and services that were once the exclusive domain of the other. This means that a broker, in addition to selling stocks and bonds, may now offer clients an array of such products and services as asset management accounts, which pool all a client's assets into a single account. Checks may then be written against the consolidated account. The intense competition between brokers and bankers has resulted in converting many clients who were simple savers into investors.

Computers are revolutionizing the securities industry: speeding information from analysts to brokers, making possible complex computations that take some of the guesswork out of forecasting, and providing a host of other services that have eliminated much drudgery for the research department and enabled brokers to expedite their clients' orders. Analysts are using microcomputers to analyze balance sheets and cash flow and give brokers fast answers to clients' questions.

Now when a client calls a broker to learn the import of a company's $15 million increase in sales, for example, the analyst can punch the figure into the computer and be back to the broker in seconds with the answer. With the time the computer saves, countless more calculations can be performed in a day. Analysts can also look farther into the future, forecasting earnings three or four years ahead by trying out many different scenarios on the computer, whereas previously earnings were forecast for only a year ahead. And analysts are using the computer's word processing capabilities to produce research reports, complete with computer-drawn graphics, that can go right to the printer, eliminating the need for a typist or artist. When a stock is faltering, the broker can use the word processing capability to write individual letters to every client who holds the stock, recommending a call to the broker to discuss alternative investments.

Virtually every broker, no matter what the size of the firm, uses a microcomputer to store information on a client's holdings. This data may be cross-referenced in a variety of useful ways: by stock, by industry, or by investment objective, for example. Some firms are creating computer programs relating to options and bond trading that will balance the potential risks and gains in a proposed deal for a particular client.

The M.B.A. is highly sought by the securities industry. Although jobs are available to individuals who have only an undergraduate degree, the competition for these positions is fierce and, quite honestly, these people are often overwhelmed by this fast-paced, high-pressured industry. However, your M.B.A. alone will not make you a highly desirable candidate. Employers—especially major firms—like to see relevant work experience, whether in sales or financial research, or some other proof of your ability to succeed.

Jobs are available in the following categories:

- **Sales**
- **Research**
- **Operations**

Jobs in the first two areas are most often filled by M.B.A. graduates. Sales work requires the right combination of an outgoing personality, high energy, and excellent judgment; research work requires disciplined analytical abilities.

Job Outlook

Job Opportunities Will Grow: Faster than average

Competition for Jobs: Keen

There are about 15,000 security analysts in the United States, compared with more than 80,000 brokers (and their ranks keep growing), making sales a considerably easier area to crack— assuming you have the required sales experience.

New Job Opportunities: The deregulation of the banking industry, the peak performances of the stock market in recent times, and the dizzying array of new options being made available to investors are creating new job opportunities in both sales and research.

Deregulation has paved the way for companies to buy up a variety of financial services and bring them all under one roof to create a financial supermarket. The first to do so was Sears, Roebuck & Company. At more than 125 Sears store locations, customers can now make deposits at Allstate Savings & Loans, purchase insurance at Allstate Insurance, buy real estate through Coldwell Banker, and purchase securities through Dean Witter Reynolds. More than 850 new brokers were hired in 1983 to work in these Sears store locations, and brokers will continue to be added as more Sears stores open financial supermarkets. J.C. Penney has since followed Sears's lead.

The fierce competition for investors' money is spurring brokerage houses to enlarge their sales and research departments to attract customers, creating more jobs for brokers and analysts.

Geographic Job Index

New York, NY, has the highest concentration of brokerage firms of any city in the United States, and most of the major firms are headquartered there, so it's the best place to find jobs in research and operations. Other cities with a high concentration of brokerage firms include Boston, MA, Philadelphia, PA, Chicago, IL, Dallas, TX, San Francisco, CA, and Los Angeles, CA. The major firms have an extensive network of branch offices (Dean Witter Reynolds, for example, has more than 325 branch offices throughout the 50 states), and even small cities have one or more brokerage offices. So you could find a job in sales almost anywhere in the country, although the field is larger, naturally, in a major metropolitan area.

Who the Employers Are

NATIONAL BROKERAGE FIRMS employ thousands in their nationwide branch offices. The biggest of them all, Merrill Lynch, employs more than 15,000 people. These firms maintain large research departments and spend millions of dollars tracking down the most attractive investments for their customers.

REGIONAL BROKERAGE FIRMS provide many of the same services offered by national firms but specialize in trading and promoting the interests of local companies. They employ fewer people than national firms in their offices (all of which are concentrated in their immediate area). Some very small brokerage firms have one office in one city only.

DISCOUNT BROKERAGE HOUSES are firms that do nothing but execute trades. They do not maintain research departments or offer advice, and their fees to investors are correspondingly lower. Many banks are forming partnerships with discount brokers so they can offer their customers discount brokerage services. Two such partnerships are Bank of America and Charles Schwab and Chase Manhattan Bank and Rose & Company. Many discount brokerage houses are national, but there are local ones as well.

COMMERCIAL BANKS have clients who are principally institutions and individuals with large sums to invest. They employ portfolio managers to handle such investments. Their staffs also include buy-side analysts, who offer purchase recommendations. (Unlike sell-side analysts, who are at securities firms that sell stock, buy-side analysts work for institutions making stock purchases.)

INSURANCE COMPANIES also hire buy-side analysts, who are responsible for advising the company about investing the huge sums of money collected as premiums from policyholders.

Major Employers

Allen & Company, New York, NY
Bear Stearns & Company, New York, NY
A.G. Becker, Inc., New York, NY
Dean Witter Reynolds, Inc., New York, NY
Donaldson Lufkin & Jenrette, Inc., New York, NY
Drexel Burnham Lambert, Inc., New York, NY

A.G. Edwards & Sons, St. Louis, MO
The First Boston Corporation, New York, NY
Goldman Sachs, New York, NY
E.F. Hutton Company, New York, NY
Kidder Peabody Company, Inc., New York, NY
Merrill Lynch Pierce Fenner & Smith, Inc., New York, NY
Morgan Stanley & Company, New York, NY
Paine Webber, New York, NY
Prudential-Bache Securities Brokers, New York, NY
L.F. Rothschild Unterberg Towbin, New York, NY
Salomon Brothers, Inc., New York, NY
The Securities Groups, New York, NY
Shearson Lehman/American Express Inc., New York, NY
Shelby Cullom Davis & Company, New York, NY
Smith Barney Harris Upham & Company, Inc., New York, NY
Spear Leeds & Kellogg, New York, NY
Stephens, Inc., Little Rock, AR
Thomson McKinnon Securities, New York, NY

How to Break into the Field

Many securities firms recruit at business schools, but you should
not depend only on this source of interviews. The surest route to an
interview is through personal contacts; the school's alumni or
placement office should be able to direct you to alumni in the
industry. If a family member, friend, or neighbor has worked
closely with a brokerage firm, don't ignore this possible entree.

If you lack any useful personal contacts, try a letter-writing
campaign. If you'd like a job as a broker, write to the account
executive recruitment office at the headquarters or to the branch
manager at locations in your area. If your interest lies in operations, write to the operations manager at the firm's headquarters. Send a carefully worded letter stating your qualifications and
requesting an interview. Enclose your résumé. Follow it up with a
phone call requesting an appointment for an interview.

International Job Opportunities

International opportunities are extremely limited. Most of the major firms have offices abroad, but they tend to hire local residents for the positions that exist there.

SALES

Brokers (also known as account executives, registered representatives, or salespeople) act as agents for people buying or selling securities. Because the performance of an account executive is crucial to the client's satisfaction and the firm's reputation, candidates are put through a rugged qualifying process at any large brokerage firm. The first hurdle is usually a general aptitude test; if you complete that successfully, you'll be interviewed by a succession of people, usually beginning with a corporate recruiter or a branch manager, who will rate your potential for success as a broker. The final hurdle will be a measurement of your sales skills in a test that includes exercises simulating problems and situations commonly faced by brokers. These involve telephone calls to prospects and relevant analytical work. Try to talk to a broker beforehand to prepare for this phase of the process.

As a beginning broker, your aim will be to build up a clientele. The best place to start is with people you know—family, friends, neighbors, members of groups or clubs to which you belong. You'll also be combing phone directories and mailing lists for names of prospective clients and spending the bulk of each day soliciting (many firms expect new brokers to make between 50 and 100 phone calls a day). While you continue to search for new business you'll be servicing your clients: keeping them abreast of their stocks' performance, executing trades, and recommending financial investments suitable to their needs and objectives.

Brokers usually specialize in one type of security, either stocks or bonds, and either in retail sales, where your clients are individuals, or institutional sales. Another specialized area is that of floor broker, who works on the floor of a stock exchange, executing the actual trades of listed stocks.

To become a broker, you must pass the licensing exam given by the New York Stock Exchange, the main regulatory body for all the exchanges; in order to take the test, you must be sponsored by a firm. The firm that hires you will put you through an intensive account executive training program and give you study guides to help you prepare for the licensing exam. During the first three months of your training, while you prepare for the exam, you'll be observing the activities of a working brokerage firm. An additional month might be spent taking courses at the firm's training center.

During the next year, you'll be a broker-in-training at a branch office, with the manager of the branch serving as your supervisor. While you're in training, you'll be paid a salary. Once the training period ends, however, you'll be working strictly on commission, so your income will depend on how many transactions you process. Since brokerage firms demand a high level of productivity (many expect to see brokers earn about $50,000 in gross commissions the first year), be prepared to work hard.

Qualifications

Personal: Self-confidence. Personality. Foresight. Drive. Persistence. Ability to influence others. The strength to withstand frequent rejection.

Professional: Ability to work comfortably with numbers. Understanding of basic business concepts. Previous sales experience preferred.

Career Paths

LEVEL	JOB TITLE	EXPERIENCE NEEDED
Entry	Sales trainee	M.B.A., sales experience helpful

LEVEL	JOB TITLE	EXPERIENCE NEEDED
2	Account executive	1 year
3	Branch manager	3-4 years
4	Regional manager	5-7 years
5	National sales manager	8+ years

Job Responsibilities

Entry Level

THE BASICS: Identifying prospective clients through mailing lists and phone directories, and making cold telephone solicitations. Answering clients' telephone queries. Reading financial publications. Processing transactions.

MORE CHALLENGING DUTIES: Advising clients on appropriate investment strategies. Keeping current clients informed of their stocks' performance by telephone or letter. Studying reports from the research department.

Moving Up

Your success depends on how hard you're willing to work—the number and quality of clients you can attract, your investment acumen, the soundness of the judgments you make on the basis of factual material from the research department, and your willingness to do more than simply take orders from your clients. It takes years to build a reputation as a broker who knows his or her business thoroughly. If you become a top performer in your branch and have managerial know-how, you may be offered the job of branch manager.

If you reach that point, you'll be required to relinquish all but a few of your clients. (You may be able to retain those with whom you have a personal relationship or those who are your biggest investors.) As a branch manager, you'll be paid a salary plus a bonus based on the amount of money the branch office brings in. In addition, you will collect commissions on any transactions you continue to make.

RESEARCH

A broker is only as successful as the company's research department. Knowing which stocks to go after and which to sell comes from listening to the presentations and reading the reports of the firm's researchers, or security analysts, who study stocks and bonds, assess their current value, and forecast their earning potential. Security analysts tend to specialize in a single industry, such as oil or steel, quickly becoming experts in their area.

Qualifications

Personal: Ability to work under pressure. Foresight. Self-confidence. Ability to trust your own instincts.

Professional: Verbal and writing skills. Keen analytical skills. Familiarity with accounting procedures. Ability to read between the lines of annual reports. Facility working with a software calc program.

Career Paths

LEVEL	JOB TITLE	EXPERIENCE NEEDED
Entry	Research assistant/ junior analyst	M.B.A.
2	Senior analyst	3+ years
3	Managing director	10 years

Job Responsibilities

Entry Level

THE BASICS: Reading financial reports. Analyzing corporate balance sheets. Number crunching. Making written recommendations to senior analysts. Assisting senior people at whatever research work needs to be done.

MORE CHALLENGING DUTIES: Accompanying senior analysts on visits to corporation officials to gather firsthand information about the company. Advising the firm's brokers on specific stocks. Fielding questions posed by brokers.

Moving Up

After a period of gaining familiarity with and expertise in a particular industry, if you demonstrate that your analyses and interpretations of trends and developments are sound, you may be promoted to senior analyst. As a senior analyst, you'll be called on to answer any difficult questions posed by brokers or their clients, and act as adviser on all stocks related to the industry in which you are expert. You'll periodically visit branch offices to deliver oral presentations, accompanied by written reports on your industry to brokers there. You'll also be accompanying institutional sales-people on their visits to lucrative accounts.

OPERATIONS

The operations department, or "back office," is where the hundreds of thousands of daily transactions made by the firm's brokers are processed and recorded. The work is divided among several groups of clerks, each group with specific responsibilities. The purchasing and sales clerks make sure that every buy matches up with a sale by studying the computer printouts that record all transactions. The main source of this information is the Securities

Industry Automation Corporation, an automated clearinghouse that is jointly owned by the New York and American Exchanges. The printouts show every buy and sale on these exchanges in a single day; in addition, this same source provides information on national trading. Firms trading on exchanges outside New York, NY, receive comparable information from other automated sources. Clerks in client services post dividends to clients' accounts and mail out monthly statements. Margin clerks keep track of clients' accounts, making sure they haven't purchased more on credit than is legally allowed. Compliance clerks ensure that transactions are completed according to all rules and regulations spelled out in the *New York Stock Exchange Constitution and Rules* book. Department heads oversee each of these services.

Securities are received and stored or transferred in a top-security area called the cage, which only a few people in the firm are allowed to enter. Cage clerks microfilm all securities and box them for storage in the vault or transfer them elsewhere to be stored.

In operations, the M.B.A. graduate will be assigned directly to a supervisory position. A supervisor is typically responsible for five to seven clerks, assigning their work, monitoring their productivity, and offering guidance when needed. From supervisor, you may advance to section head; here you act as a liaison between departments and handle day-to-day problems that might prevent the department from functioning smoothly and effectively.

ADDITIONAL INFORMATION

Salaries

SALES commissions vary with the type of security and the size of the transaction. Retail brokers collect between 30 and 40 percent of the fee that the firm charges for each transaction; institutional brokers collect somewhat less—around 15 percent—because large blocks of securities are being traded. For brokers who bring in a high volume of business, there are numerous incentives, such as free trips and raises in commission. The income potential is unlimited, and some brokers gross in excess of $1 million a year in commissions.

RESEARCH salaries range from $30,000 a year for entry-level M.B.A.s to six-figure incomes for managing directors. The analysts are rated by the brokers on the basis of the quality and depth of their research and their record of success. These ratings are carefully considered when analysts are up for their biannual bonuses.

OPERATIONS salaries for supervisors with M.B.A. degrees start at $30,000 a year plus bonuses.

Working Conditions

Hours: A broker's day usually begins at 8 A.M., in time to read the papers and financial journals and talk with the research department before the exchanges open at nine. Brokers often leave the office once trading ends at 4 P.M. Operations work is usually nine to five, with overtime when trading is heavy. Supervisors and section heads put in slightly longer hours, perhaps eight-thirty to six, to catch up with administrative details or attend meetings. Research analysts work the longest hours, typically past 7 P.M.

Environment: Junior brokers, clerks, and junior analysts work in bullpen arrangements. Senior brokers, operations managers, and senior analysts have private offices. Typically, those in sales enjoy the plushest surroundings.

Workstyle: Sales personnel spend a great deal of time on the phone, either speaking with established clients or soliciting new business. Institutional salespeople may wine and dine big clients after normal business hours. Clerks and operations supervisors spend nearly all their time on paperwork, but operations managers may be in meetings up to half of each day. Research is also a desk job; the study of financial statements involves using the microcomputer to arrive at various indicators of a company's financial status: asset/debt ratio, sales/inventory ratio, sales/debt ratio. You will meet at least once a week with other members of your research team.

Travel: Opportunities to travel are nonexistent for brokers and operations staffs. Regional and national sales managers visit branch offices frequently. As a research analyst, how much you travel and how far you go depends on the industry you cover. If you specialize in an industry the center of which is in your home area, out-of-town trips may be infrequent.

Internships

Many firms are willing to take on M.B.A. students as interns or as temporary employees during summers. You should apply for these positions just as you would for a full-time job. Although some firms announce through campus placement offices that they are looking for interns and temporary help, you should also investigate opportunities on your own.

Because of the growing awareness that on-the-job training is a better test of your abilities than academic experience alone, some large firms are recruiting M.B.A. graduates for intensive, long-term internships that expose them to all areas of the industry. These programs accept candidates on the assumption that these individuals will become full-time employees if they like the industry and can handle the work.

Recommended Reading

BOOKS

The Money Game by Adam Smith, Vintage: 1976

The Money Messiahs by Norman King, Coward-McCann: 1983

Stealing from the Rich: The Story of the Swindle of the Century by David McClintick, Quill Publications: 1983

DIRECTORIES

Broker-Dealer Directory (annual), Securities and Exchange Commission, Washington, DC

Security Dealers of North America (semiannual), Standard & Poor, New York, NY

Who's Who in the Securities Industry (annual), Economist Publishing Company, Chicago, IL

PERIODICALS

Barron's (weekly), Dow Jones & Company, 22 Cortlandt Street, New York, NY 10007

Business Week (weekly), McGraw-Hill Publications, 1221 Avenue of the Americas, New York, NY 10020

Dun's Business Month (monthly), Dun & Bradstreet Corporation, 875 Third Avenue, New York, NY 10022

Financial World (bimonthly), Macro Communications, Inc., 1250 Broadway, New York, NY 10001

Forbes (biweekly), 60 Fifth Avenue, New York, NY 10011

Fortune (biweekly), Time & Life Building, Rockefeller Center, New York, NY 10020

Institutional Investor (monthly), 488 Madison Avenue, New York, NY 10022

Investment Dealers Digest (weekly), 150 Broadway, New York, NY 10038

Money (monthly), Time & Life Building, Rockefeller Center, New York, NY 10020

The Wall Street Journal (daily), Dow Jones & Company, 22 Cortlandt Street, New York, NY 10007

Weekly Bond Buyer (weekly), Bond Buyer, 1 State Street Plaza, New York, NY 10004

Professional Associations

Financial Analyst Federation
1633 Broadway
New York, NY 10019

National Association of Security Dealers
2 World Trade Center
New York, NY 10048

Securities Industry Association
120 Broadway
New York, NY 10271

INTERVIEWS

Assistant Vice President, Research
L.F. Rothschild Unterberg Tobin, New York, NY

I was a triple in college—history, political science, and economics—and I hasten to add that I managed to do that major in economics without taking any courses in mathematics. I definitely did fall into that category of women who have a negative reaction to numbers. Upon graduation I worked for the Corporation for Public Broadcasting in their human resources development. Part of my responsibility was monitoring the employment and portrayal of women and minorities in public broadcasting. That necessitated doing quarterly reports to a congressional committee, and I had to start compiling employment figures, statistics—and there was math staring at me! I later became responsible for the departmental budget, which was rather substantial as our department was responsible for handing out training grants throughout the system. I quickly discovered there was nothing to be frightened about.

I enjoyed that for a while, but got somewhat tired of the nonprofit orientation. It's not very insightful, but the way I ended up in securities was to look in Washington, DC, and to find out what kind of private oriented enterprises there were. And there were not many. I won't say "securities" bounced right out of the phone book—but it was the only industry I could see getting into without a great deal of difficulty. I had invested with some success on my own and found it interesting, so I investigated the various brokerage firms in Washington, and found that Ferris and Company, which is a fine regional house in Washington, had a superior, intensive training program.

Once I was in securities I found out that if I wanted to go beyond the basic retail broker status, I had to have a graduate degree. And that's why I went back to school to get an M.B.A. I went to George Washington University while I was still working at Ferris. Because the only management position available at a regional house would be a branch manager, and that certainly was out of the question with my few years of experience, and not having built and enormous clientele book, I decided to come back to New York, which is my native state.

I never liked pure sales and never did cold calling, and quite frankly was uncomfortable with pure commission as a source of income. So I found myself getting more and more involved in the total financial picture of my clients, which gave me a greater level of security in terms of what I was or was not doing with their money. And that was quite suitable experience for the posiion I now hold in Rothschild's research department. I'm in what's known as portfolio research, and that job entails essentially being a broker to our brokers. They submit their client portfolio with the appropriate investment objective information, and we analyze the portfolio or develop a portfolio to meet the client's needs. The beauty of this is that it gives the client excellent service, because this is done at no additonal fee, and I have no vested interest in whether the broker buys or sells. I make decisions on a needs basis for the client versus a need basis for the broker.

The bottom line about having the M.B.A. is that it helped me get the job. I don't know that I use more that 10 percent of what I learned. The program that I was involved in was more qualitative than quantitative, which I frankly liked, and I think an awful lot of large corporations are coming to the conclusion that the quantitative programs are great in the short term, but they're finding that the long-term objectives of many corporations are being sacrificed. That's a consideration one should look at seriously when picking an M.B.A. program. I also think one should work before going for a graduate degree. Although there are hordes of recruiters on campuses these days, and M.B.A.s are still pulling in a fairly nice salary for an initial job, I do think that the allure of the degree without work experience is rapidly dissipating. More and more employers are saying that without experience what you've learned means nothing to you because you haven't been able to apply it while you learned it. The M.B.A. was more a premium degree when I got it than it is today, but it's a question of having the degree to get the door open now.

Sixty to 70 percent of my day is spent talking to brokers, responding to questions on particular stocks about whether they're appropriate for specific clients, looking at portfolios, and going to meetings with other analysts to look at companies or to discuss the general market outlook. The balance of the time is spent with my clients, which is the icing on the cake. I enjoy my salary compensation, and then can do as much commission business as I want. I'm constantly reading research reports of other firms or independent research organizations, and company annual reports, and doing spread sheets on earnings projections. I also function as a conduit between the specialized analysts who cover specific industries and the broker for those securities that our firms covers on a regular basis. When we're talking about companies that are not regularly followed, that's when I have to look at them.

I like the sense of power in this job. It's really rather heady to have brokers who've been on Wall Street for 30 years have to ask me if it's okay to by or sell something. But I also enjoy the research end. I have found—much to my surprise over the years—that numbers are not intimidating at all. It gives me the opportunity to be both a broker for those clients that I do handle without being compelled to trade in their accounts to make my living. And I like being of assistance to the brokers because, although I don't have a vested interest in whether they buy or sell, over the long term if you do a portfolio structure that is appropriate for their client they keep the client. It's not a question of perhaps buying one or two stocks that don't turn out so the client goes to some other broker. If you can do a total picture so that no single security will make or break them, they're going to keep their portfolio with you.

Leah Pfeffer
Administrative Manager, Institutional Sales
Dean Witter Reynolds, Inc., New York, NY

My first profession was teaching—I have a B.S. and an M.S. in education—but after three years at the head of a third-grade class-room, I was ready for something new. I was interested in business (and I must admit I was ready to work with adults), but beyond that I didn't have a clear idea of where to start looking. An employment agency sent me to interview for a position as a sales assistant with a brokerage house. I knew little about either securities or sales, but the job interested me and it met my two basic requirements—it didn't require typing and I wouldn't be taking a cut in pay by switching jobs. I didn't get that job, but I found what I had been looking for. I applied for other sales assistant openings and wound up at Thomson McKinnon. That was in 1968.

I learned a great deal about securities. The firm sent me to the New York Institute of Finance, which prepared me to take (and pass) the registered representative exam with the New York Stock Exchange. But I knew I didn't want to be an assistant forever. I pursued sales, moving to a small brokerage house called Hirsch and Company. Few woman were in sales at that time. In fact, I have wondered if the primary reason I got that job was because I was interviewed by one ot the few female partners then in the business.

I received no formal training—I was given a phone and a desk, and I was on my own! Building a client base was tough. I found myself in a bear market with few products to sell. At the time, brokers dealt mainly with stocks. We sold some bonds, but the options market was really just starting. Today, a broker has much more to work with.

The bad part of being a broker is that you are always on the job. Wherever you go, whomever you meet, one thing is foremost in your mind—making client contacts. I did a lot of cold calling. I did hit on a trick to make contacts, however. I would go through the phone book, calling everyone with the name of Pfeffer. By playing up the coincidence of our names, I could break the ice, and often people would talk to me because of the connection.

The firm went out of business, which gave me a chance to reevaluate my goals. I came to the conclusion that I would be happier not selling. I was not bad at selling, but the job just didn't fit my personality. I went back to Loeb Rhoades (now a part of Shearson Lehman/American Express), handling day-to-day, administrative details as a supervisor. After four years, I moved to Bache Halsey Stuart, Inc. (now Prudential Bache), where I spent another four years as manager of marketing and support services in the institutional sales department.

In institutional sales, we sell our product—our research—to major clients, such as bank trust departments and large pension funds. I was responsible for discovering what our clients needed in terms of the research itself and what they expected in terms of its presentation. Some wanted a broad analysis; others asked for more specific information. The data must be easily understandable and, above all, must be timely.

I left Bache after four years, moving to Dean Witter Reynolds. I still work with institutional sales, but am more involved with overseeing department functions. Institutional sales is now getting into new areas. Electronic transmittal of data is speeding our delivery to customers. And we are now looking into closed circuit television. With it, we will be able to contact our clients directly; our research analysts and salespeople won't travel, but may make all their analytical presentations and sales calls on television. Your clients always expect you to have a crystal ball. Not so long ago, clients wanted forecasts for the coming year or two; now they want predictions five years in advance! As research techniques become more sophisticated, our forecasts seem to be getting much more accurate, but of course room for error remains.

Although I do not do actual selling, my sales background has helped me immensely. I understand the pressures on our salespeople. And in a sense, I still do some selling—not to the clients, but to the salespeople. I tell them what we can supply to clients, and I motivate them to sell our services.

I am a member of the Financial Women's Association of New York, an organization that includes women from many different financially oriented professions. I enjoy meeting other professional women to compare notes and exchange information. And, as you progress in your career, networking is important.

I have also supplemented work experience with an M.B.A. I went at night, taking six years to complete the degree. As you can tell, I wasn't in a hurry! The best place to learn is on the job, but I felt I needed the M.B.A. to remain competitive. So far, having the degree has not made a difference in my job; however, if I decide to look for another job, it may be valuable. The M.B.A. is simply becoming more common. In order to compete against other advanced-degree holders, you need it.

BIBLIOGRAPHY

MBA Answer Book: A Career Guide for the Person Who Means Business by Mark O'Brian, Prentice-Hall: 1984

MBA Career by Bob Hisrich and Eugene Bronstein, Barron's Educational Series: 1983

M.B.A. Degree by Eppen et. al., Chicago Review Press: 1979

MBA: How to Prepare for, Apply for, and Derive Maximum Advantage from Graduate Study in Management by Pat C. Lafitte, Barnes & Noble: 1981

MBA's Dictionary by Daniel Oran and Jay M. Shafritz, Prentice-Hall: 1983

Should You Get an MBA? by Albert P. Hegyi, President, and Staff of Associates of MBA Executives, Inc., Prentice-Hall: 1982

INDEX

NOTES

NOTES

NOTES

NOTES

NOTES

NOTES

NOTES

NOTES

NOTES

NOTES

NOTES

NOTES

NOTES

✻ ─────────────────────────────

─────────────────────────────

NOTES